LOST OREGON STREETCARS

RICHARD THOMPSON

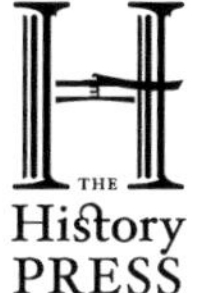

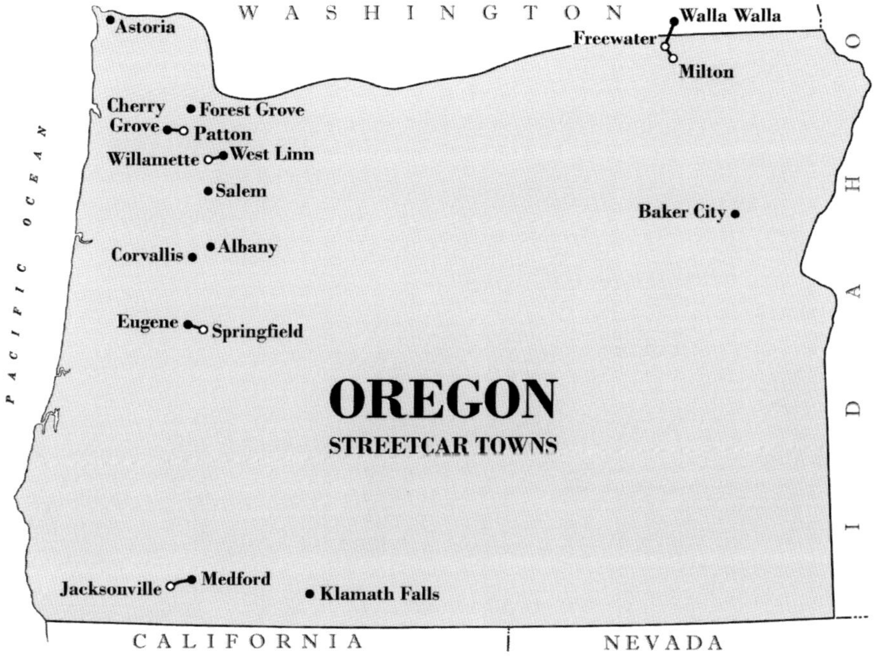

Eleven Oregon cities (not counting Portland) had street railways at one time, including Albany, Astoria, Baker City, Cherry Grove, Corvallis, Eugene, Forest Grove, Klamath Falls, Medford, Salem and West Linn. Four additional towns—Freewater, Jacksonville, Milton and Springfield—were connected by electric railway lines extending from nearby cities. Willamette was included in this last group until it was absorbed into West Linn in 1916. *Map by author.*

Published by The History Press
Charleston, SC
www.historypress.net

First published 2017

Manufactured in the United States

ISBN 9781467136853

Library of Congress Control Number: 2016950692

Notice: The information in this book is true and complete to the best of our knowledge. It is offered without guarantee on the part of the author or The History Press. The author and The History Press disclaim all liability in connection with the use of this book.

To my father,
Orval N. Thompson (1914–2002)

CONTENTS

ACKNOWLEDGEMENTS

I say this with every book I write, but it is still so true: I am forever indebted to my late friends William K. "Bill" Hayes and G. Charles "Chuck" Bukowsky for their help and encouragement over the more than forty years spent gathering materials for my books. I also wish to thank the late William R. "Mitch" Mitchum, Robert "Bob" Potts and Ebbert "Bert" Webber for sharing images from their collections so that they might reach a wider audience.

I want to express my sincere gratitude to Ed Austin, Paul Class, Tom Dill, Brian McCamish, Robert I. Melbo, Rick Minor, Mark Moore, Mary Jo Morelli, Donald R. Nelson, Kathryn Notson, Ron Preston and Arlen Sheldrake for sending much-needed pictures and information. I am always impressed by the camaraderie that exists among those who share a love for local history.

I am also grateful for the professional assistance received from Ryan Finn, my production editor, and Megan Laddusaw, my commissioning editor, at The History Press; Linda Ellsworth of the Linn Genealogical Society; Winn Herrschaft of the Washington County Historical Society; and Cheryl Roffe of the Lane County Historical Society.

Finally, I am very grateful to my friend and fellow trolley enthusiast Mark Kavanagh for diligently fact-checking the manuscript. Mark gave up time during a family holiday to double-check a few last-minute additions.

All the material used in this book is from the author's collection unless otherwise noted. More information can be found on his website (http://vintagetrolleys.com).

INTRODUCTION

By the turn of the twentieth century, the street railway had become a vital part of urban transportation. Naturally, this phenomenon arrived first in large cities, but it was soon desired by smaller municipalities as well. A locality's pride in achieving its own streetcar line is apparent in postcards prominently featuring streetcars trundling down Main Street.

The first—and, for that matter, last—streetcars in Oregon ran in the largest city, Portland. That history has been told before by this author, as well as others. This volume tells the story of the lost Oregon streetcars that operated in smaller towns between 1888 and 1933. They were the unsung heroes that brought modern transit, with all of its benefits and drawbacks, to the hinterlands. As will be seen, the forgotten history of those streetcar lines, successful or otherwise, is every bit as diverse and fascinating as Portland's.

As elsewhere, the earliest streetcars to appear in small towns were horse-drawn. They were essentially omnibuses (or, to be more western, stages) riding on tracks. Early on, it had been discovered that horses could pull a heavier load, and at a faster pace, over steel rails. This would be nowhere more appreciated than in towns where paved roads were the exception. During rainy weather, muddy, rutted streets became impassible—except, of course, for those lucky enough to live in places that offered the convenience of a streetcar. In time, street railways came to be regarded as a necessity, like electricity or plumbing.

Since horses were expensive to feed and house, and could not reasonably be expected to pull a streetcar more than three or four miles, other forms of motive power were soon under consideration. In Albany, when mechanized mass transit was introduced, it was in the form of former horsecars pulled by a small steam locomotive clad in a wooden body designed to look like a streetcar. These "dummy" locomotives offered more speed and power than horsecars, and they could travel long distances. Yet they were soon replaced by an even more efficient kind of streetcar.

The majority of Oregon's smaller streetcar systems were incorporated in the 1890s, by which time it had become apparent that the most effective form of streetcar was the electric car, or trolley, so-called because their overhead poles "trolled" the wire for power. Systems that were able to make the transition from horse, or steam, to electric operation survived the longest. Trolleys lasted more than thirty years in Eugene, Salem and West Linn and for more than twenty in Albany and Milton-Freewater. In contrast, the streetcars that never evolved beyond horse power vanished from Klamath Falls in four years, from Corvallis in six and from Baker City in nine.

Not surprisingly, the street railways with "deeper pockets" fared best. The Albany, Eugene, Salem and West Linn systems became part of the vast Southern Pacific Railroad, and the streetcars in Astoria, Milton and Freewater belonged to the Pacific Power and Light Company. Smaller towns appealed to outside investors, as well as to local banking, real estate and utility businesses, for financial backing, but they were not as successful in attracting capital.

Some Oregon street railways were exceptions in that their primary goal was to provide a link to other places rather than to move people around town. The towns of Milton and Freewater never had city streetcars; however, the interurban from Walla Walla, Washington, served a similar, if less frequent, purpose by providing transportation in these close-together towns. In Medford, the city trolley line grew by merging with an older steam railroad to Jacksonville.

The streetcars in Forest Grove and in West Linn were conceived as what we might now call shuttles. Forest Grove's trolley connected with a mainline railroad station that was outside city limits, while the railway in West Linn was designed to carry workers to an electric power plant and nearby factories. Unlike other small-town systems, the railways in both Forest Grove and West Linn were electric from the start.

The steam railroad in Cherry Grove was the most unique of all. Its operators desired a trolley but avoided the expense of electrifying the line by ordering the first battery-powered streetcar in the West. It supplanted an earlier gasoline automobile fitted with steel rail wheels and was eventually replaced by another gasoline rail car. But until the late 1920s, Oregon's only storage battery streetcar reigned supreme in this tiny town.

Most of Oregon's small-town streetcar systems ceased operation (sometimes converting to buses) during the 1920s, by which time they had been deemed unprofitable. The one system that might have outlasted others, in Astoria, was destroyed in a 1922 fire.

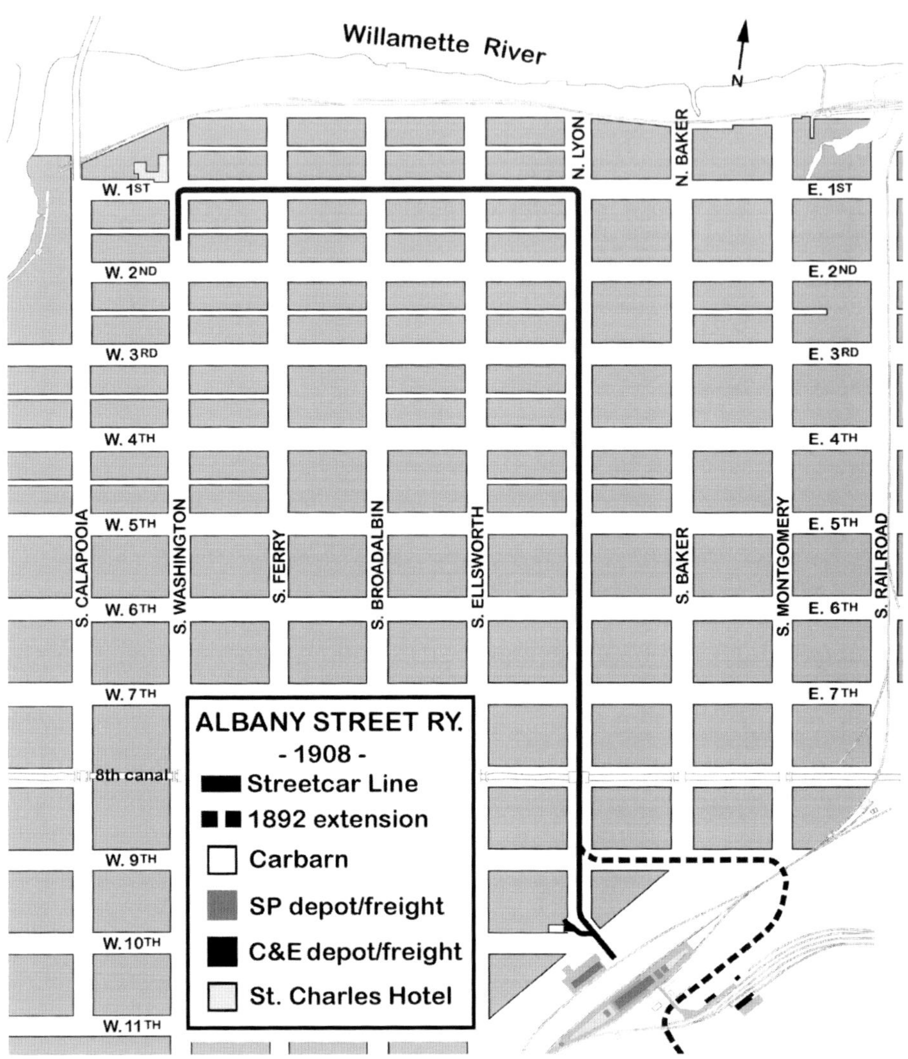

From 1889 to 1918, the Albany Street Railway operated the streetcar line shown on this map. It ran from the train depots at the foot of South Lyon Street to West First Avenue and Washington Street in the central business district. The one addition to the system, shown with dashed lines, was a half-mile extension to the Children's Orphan Home in the Goltra Park Addition, which was in use from 1892 until about 1900. The short spur to the left led to the horsecar and steam dummy carbarn (not used during the trolley years). *Map by author.*

Chapter 1

ALBANY, 1889–1918

Albany's street railway began with a one-mile horsecar system that ran from the Oregon and California (O&C) Railroad depot to the downtown business district by way of Lyon Street and First Avenue. When completed, its downtown terminus was next to the St. Charles Hotel on First Avenue and Washington Street.

On August 30, 1889, the Albany Street Railway's inaugural trip from the O&C station was reported in the pages of the *Albany Democrat* with all the hyperbole typical of the time. Interestingly, this account indicates that more than one car was planned and that they were to be slightly longer than the horsecars in Portland:

> *At 9:37 Monday the wheels of a street car and the rails of a line met for the first time in Albany, in the presence of several hundred people. It promises to be the beginning of a new era in this gem city of the Valley. The move has been made and the city must now keep up with the cars. The people of Albany are proud of their new cars. Manufactured by AJ Anslyn, of this city, they are the equal if not the superior of any cars in Oregon. In matter of detail and finish they show fine workmanship. Mr. Anslyn superintended their construction. The Albany Iron Works manufactured the wheels and other iron work. Mr. George Vassalo did the painting and JF Whiting the lettering. The cars are twelve feet inside, being half a foot longer than the Morrison Street cars in Portland. The cars have been housed for the present, and it will be several days before they will be run regularly.*

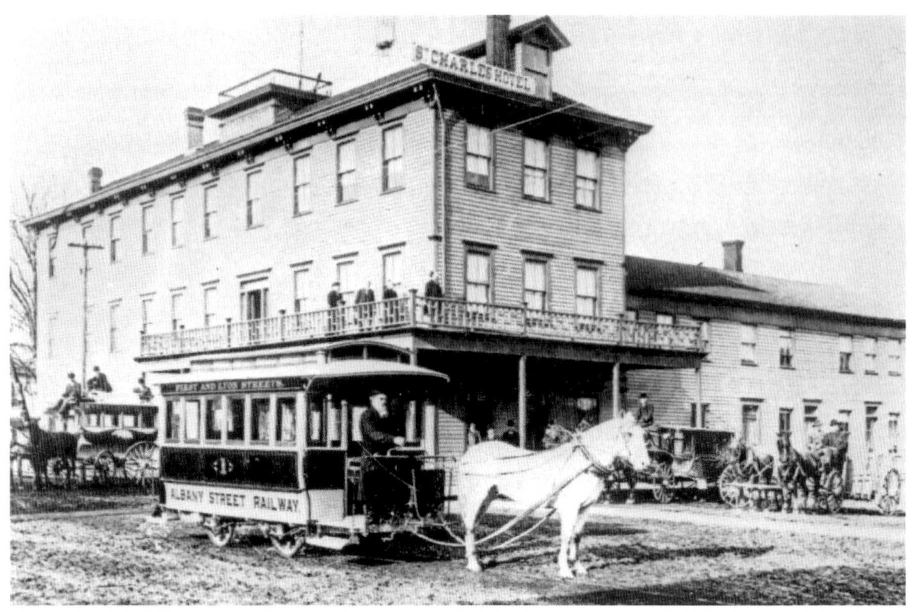

Albany's first streetcar was built by the Albany Iron Works in 1889. This picture was taken at First and Washington in front of the Saint Charles Hotel during the 1890s. *Author's collection.*

> *At 2 o' clock the magnates of the road and newspaper men were given a ride over the line of the road, much to their joy and admiration of the car, railroad track and everything concerned with the matter. The Democrat hopes to see these street cars a paying thing from the start.*[1]

Construction of the O&C main line through Albany had been highly political—railroad president Ben Holliday having been motivated by a $50,000 subsidy raised by local business leaders. Nevertheless, its impact on the city was undeniable; the arrival of the railroad in December 1870 laid the groundwork for Albany's rise in industrial and economic status as the "Hub City" of the Willamette Valley.

The original wood-frame O&C passenger depot was a combination station, hotel and restaurant surrounded by parklike grounds. The freight depot was next door. The station served the city very well from its opening in 1871 until it was moved two blocks west, to the bottom of Lyon Street, in 1908. The recycled building continued in use for many years as the Depot Hotel. A handsome new Union Depot, still in use by Amtrak today, replaced the original station.

In 1887, the Oregon Pacific Railroad (OPR) bestowed Albany its second railroad connection. The OPR had been organized in 1880 by Colonel

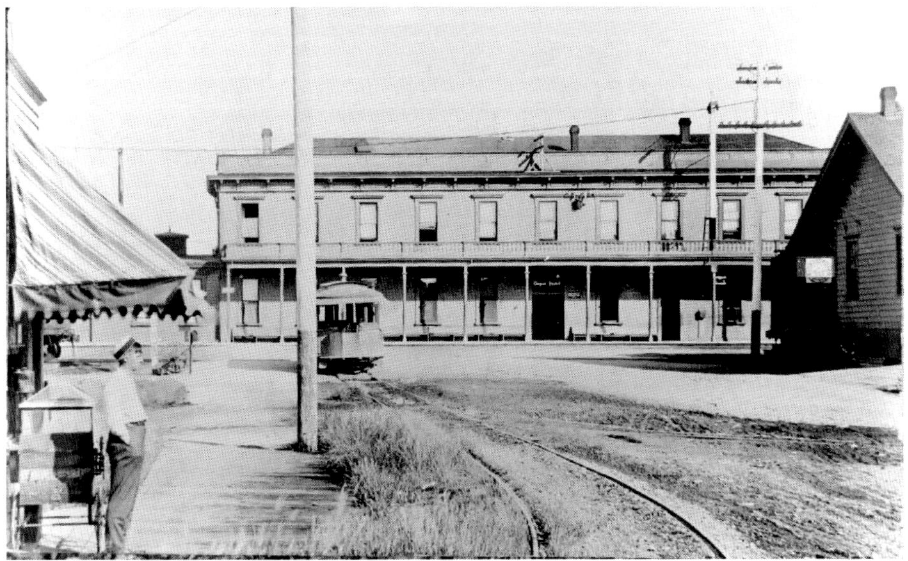

The Albany Street Railway horsecar waits next to the original Oregon and California Railroad depot and hotel, circa 1906. At left, a man stands beside a popcorn machine in front of the cigar and fruit store. On the right is the freight depot. *Robert Potts Collection.*

Thomas Edgenton Hogg, a Confederate veteran who became an Oregon businessman and railroad promoter. His ambitious dream of establishing a transcontinental railroad from the Pacific Ocean to the East Coast would not be realized, yet before going bankrupt in 1890, he completed a line from Yaquina Bay, through Corvallis and Albany, to the Cascade Mountains town of Idanha. For a time, the unlucky colonel staved off the inevitable financial disaster brought on by the sinking of two of his ocean liners at Newport (some said they were sabotaged) by making a show of "operating" his railroad over the Cascades. Under the terms of an agreement with the U.S. government, Hogg would qualify for large land grants if he built a railroad through the Cascades. So, he disassembled a boxcar, hauled it up the Santiam Pass and used mules to pull it back and forth over an isolated segment of track.

Even though the mule-powered transcontinental railroad was a failure, Hogg left a legacy for Albany by opening a new market for regional lumber and agricultural products. In 1907, the line from Yaquina became the SP subsidiary Corvallis and Eastern Railroad (C&E). As fate would have it, the C&E survived much longer than the Albany Street Railway that served it.

Albany was the first small city in the state to mechanize its streetcar system. The railway added a wood-burning steam "dummy," a small

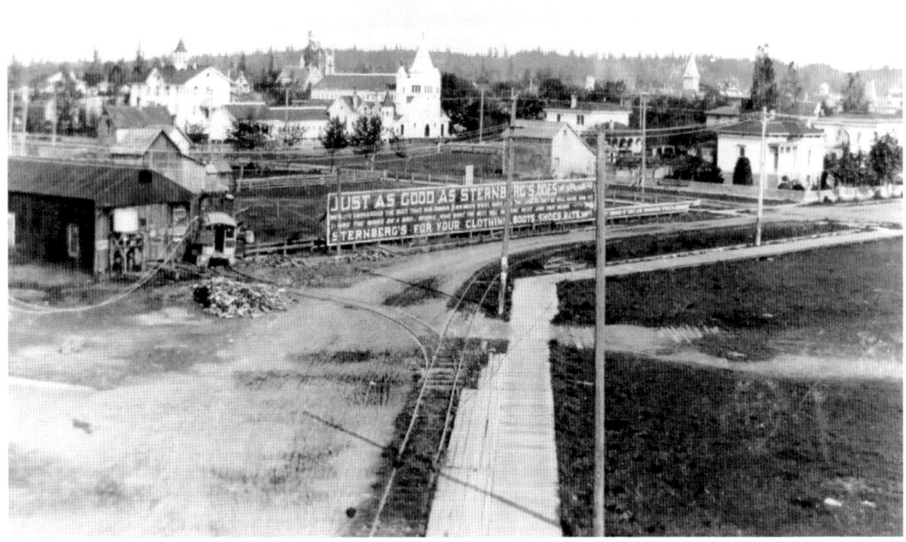

The Albany Street Railway carbarn on Lyon Street, circa 1890. In the background is the original St. Mary's Catholic Church. In 1908, the Depot Hotel moved to the vacant land behind the "Just as Good as Sternberg's" billboard. *Robert Potts Collection.*

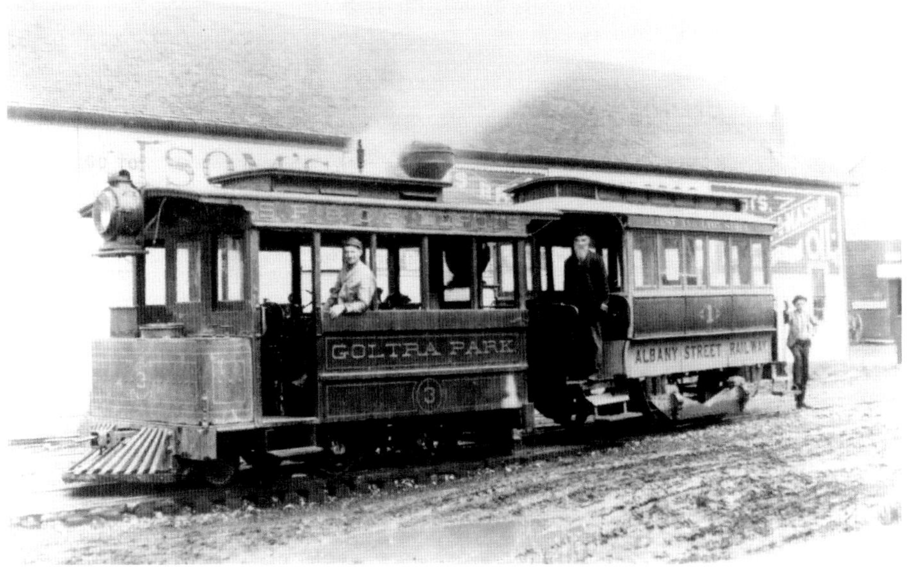

Steam Motor No. 3, pulling horsecar No. 1, in front of the wholesale fruit and produce market at the Washington Street terminus. *Author's collection.*

locomotive housed in a streetcar-like body, to pull car No. 1. Procurement of this attractive steam streetcar had been the idea of banker and real estate developer William H. Goltra, who was also vice-president of the Albany Street Railway.

In 1892, a half-mile southern extension to Goltra Park was added to the street railway. It connected with the existing line at Eight Avenue and Lyon Streets, in front of the Albany Brewing Company. The new tracks were laid in a wide arc, avoiding most railroad reserve land while passing between the O&C and OPR depots. The southern terminus, at present-day Southwest Queen Avenue and Marion Street, was near the orphan home run by the Ladies Aid Society. With this, Albany briefly had two streetcar lines.

The steam dummy was put to use on the extension, which was never electrified. Unfortunately, this marvel of the industrial age proved expensive to operate, and when it fell into disrepair, the decision was made to abandon both it and the branch to Goltra Park.

Surprisingly, this was not the end of Albany's experiment with steam-powered transit. In 1895, according to the *Jacksonville Review*, the Albany Street Railway purchased a secondhand 2-4-2T locomotive from the Rogue River Valley Railway (see chapter on Medford and Jacksonville). The locomotive, manufactured in 1891 by the H.K. Porter Company as a 2-4-2T, was rebuilt to a 0-4-2T configuration in Albany and used to pull a standard railroad coach. Engines of this type, sometimes called "dinkies," carried an onboard water supply and so did not require tenders. Evidently, this small locomotive and coach were no more reliable than their predecessor, though, because horsecar No. 1 was kept in reserve to augment them. In fact, according to local lore, Albany's street railway returned to horse power for a time:

> *"Old Charlie" was a white horse, and he was in the streetcar business. "Old Charlie" pulled Albany's one-line streetcar. He didn't start the business, nor did he finish it, but while he plodded the streets from 1900 to 1906, "Old Charlie" was known to every resident and visitor. He was Albany's most popular and best known character.*
>
> *Albany's streetcar dates back ten years before "Old Charlie" came upon the scene. In 1888–89, tracks were laid from the railroad depot, at the present location, northward on Lyon Street to First, and then westward five blocks to the turn-around at First and Washington. Three years later tracks were extended from the depot southward to the orphaned childrens* [sic] *home in Sunrise, located a few blocks south of the present Five-Corners Grocery store* [now a Circle K market].

> *The first* [mechanized] *streetcar was pulled by a small steam engine, operated by J.E. "Judd" Ross. It served hotel patrons and travelling men (drummers) who came to Albany by rail. The car met all trains and as Albany then was quite a railroad center the little car line was fairly busy. Salesmen and out-of-town shoppers would ride the car to the stores on First Street, disembark at the Russ House or Revere Hotel along the way, or ride all the way to the end of the line to the St. Charles Hotel or Albany Rooming House. The fare was five cents.*
>
> *In the course of time it became necessary to take the engine off the run. Some old-time writers claim that the steam engine needed repairs. Other writers claim that "strange" steam engine caused such confusion and excitement among carriage and wagon horses that run-away teams were making travel practically unsafe in downtown Albany. At this point "Judd" Ross decided to use horse power to operate the streetcar. "Old Charlie" was chosen for the job. That was in 1900. "Old Charlie" proved such a success that the steam locomotive was never returned to service.*
>
> *For almost four years, "Old Charlie" and "Judd" Ross made the run nine times daily. Albany was growing, business increased and a larger car was needed for the line. This car was pulled by two horses. "Old Charlie" gained a partner. When he became too old, another horse took his place and he was demoted to pulling a mail truck from the depot to the post office.*[2]

At this point Albany, and its struggling street railway, became of interest to Alvadore Welch, an enterprising electrical engineer who dreamed of building an electric interurban railroad from Portland to San Francisco. To this end, he bought the streetcar systems in Albany, Salem and Eugene and began arranging franchises for an electric line between those cities and Portland. On September 26, 1907, his Eugene and Eastern Railway Company restored streetcar service to Eugene with a new electrified system of his design. On December 31, 1908, his company—now renamed the Portland, Eugene and Eastern Railway (PE&E)—purchased the Albany Street Railway. On May 5, 1912, the PE&E acquired the street railway in Salem. In 1913, not long after E.H. Harriman, president of the Southern Pacific Railroad (SP), took notice, Welch began building south from Eugene. In 1912, the SP bought the heavily mortgaged PE&E and its small-town streetcar affiliates. Robert E. Strahorn was named president. In 1915, the Southern Pacific dropped the PE&E name and replaced it with Southern Pacific Lines. The Oregon interurban railway was also known as the Red Electric Lines because of

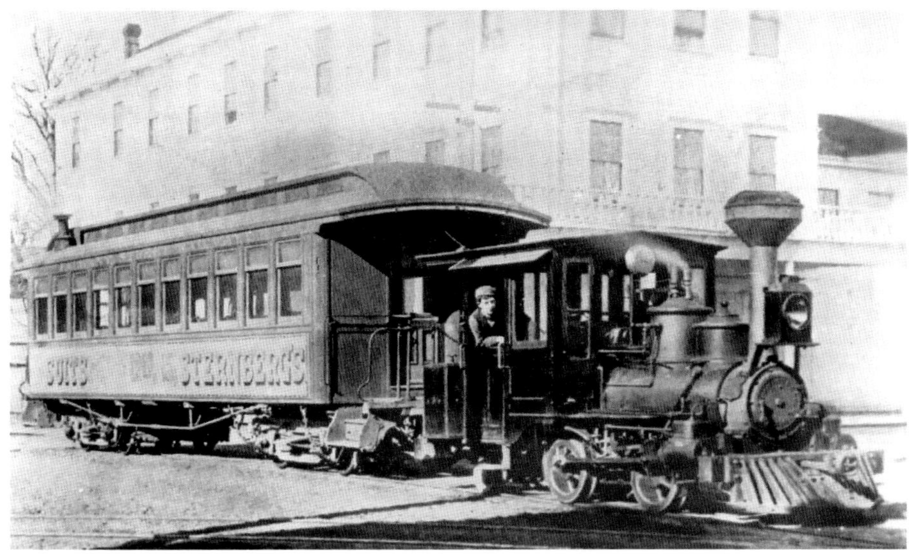

Albany's second street railway locomotive and coach, in front of the St. Charles Hotel at First and Washington Streets, circa 1900. *Robert Potts Collection.*

the color of its cars. Their bright-red livery was similar to that used by the railroad's Pacific Electric streetcars in Los Angeles.

As it happened, the SP already had strong competition from an electric railway whose tracks paralleled its proposed route through the Willamette Valley. On May 14, 1906, Thomas S. Brooks, Henry L. Corbett and R.W. Lewis had incorporated the Oregon Electric (OE) Railway. On New Year's Day 1908, electric OE trains began operating between Portland and Salem. Two years later, the OE was purchased by "Empire Builder" James J. Hill, who added it to a corporate family that included the Spokane, Portland and Seattle; the Great Northern; and the Northern Pacific Railways.

Latecomer SP caught up with its rivals by electrifying existing trackage, becoming one of the few railroads in the nation to convert branch steam railroad lines into an electric interurban network. Within four years, Albany was caught up in a railroad war. As the main lines of both companies came through the city, the PE&E used a local streetcar in an attempt to halt OE construction:

> *Placing a streetcar across the intersection of its line with the Oregon Electric until it could secure an injunction the Portland, Eugene and Eastern stopped track-laying on the Oregon Electric in this city tonight.*
>
> *The Oregon Electric track is laid on Fifth street to Lyon street, where it crosses the city line of the Portland, Eugene & Eastern. A crew planned*

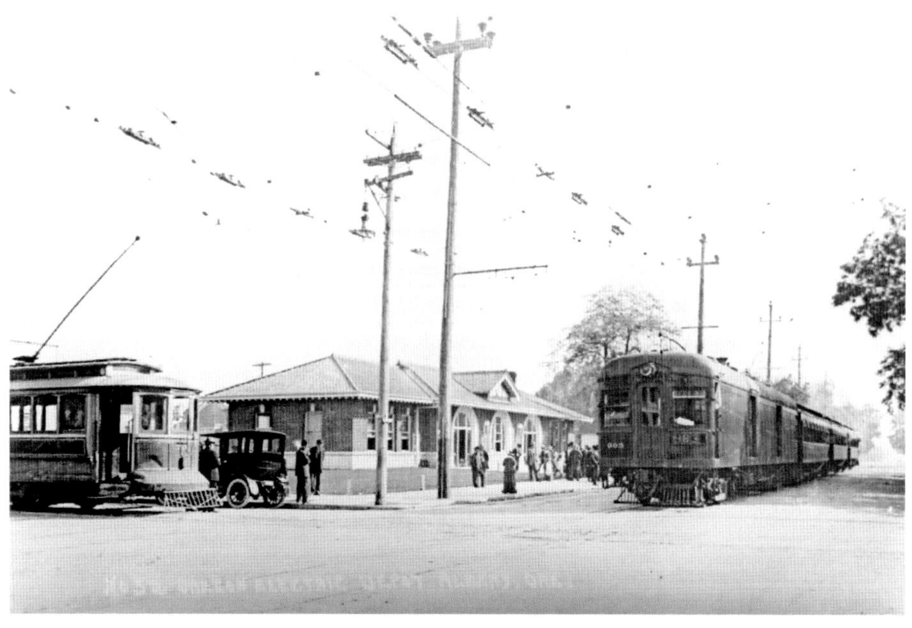

Streetcar No. 70 meets an Oregon Electric Railway special, headed by baggage motor No. 903, at the Albany depot on Fifth Avenue and Lyon Street. *Warren Wing Collection.*

> *to cut through the Portland, Eugene & Eastern track and fix the crossing during the night, so as not to stop traffic. At 6:30 o'clock tonight the car stopped square over the intersection and still stands there. An hour later a temporary injunction was secured to prevent the Oregon Electric from cutting through the crossing.*
>
> *County Judge Duncan in issuing the injunction refused to make it for a longer period than one day. This will expire tomorrow night unless renewed tomorrow.*[3]

Backers of the OE might have felt vindicated when a careless move put the city streetcar out of commission for several days in September 1912:

> *Albany will have no streetcar service for three or four days because of an accident which happened at 5 o'clock last evening. when workmen on the Oregon Electric let one of their power wires fall on the Portland, Eugene & Eastern trolley at the intersection of the two lines at Fifth and Lyon streets. The Oregon Electric wire carried 1300 volts and the trolley wire only 500, and the contact burned out the armature in the machine in the local electric plant which furnishes power for the streetcar system. It will require three or four days to secure a new armature and repair the carnage.*

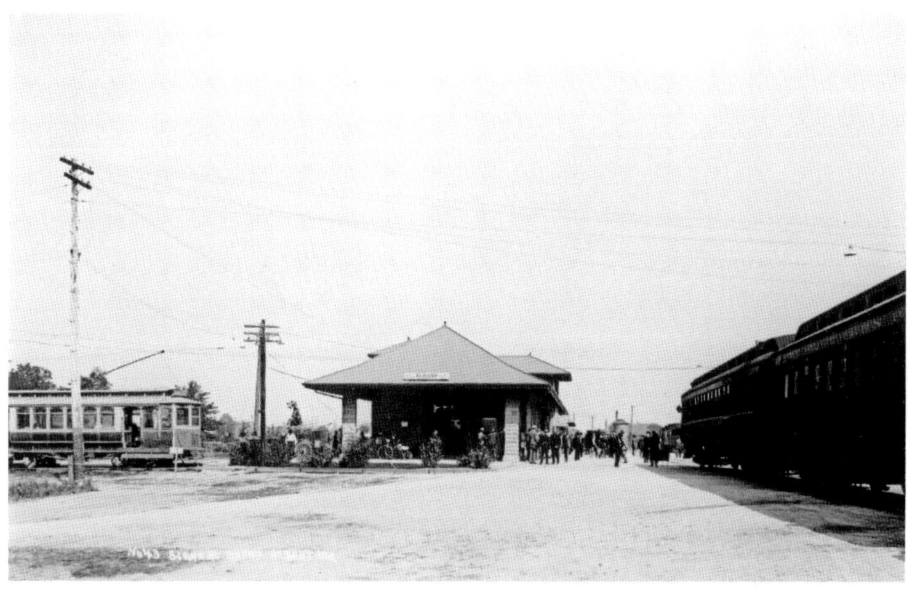

The trolley waiting in front of the Southern Pacific station was one of five "California"-style cars purchased from the Pacific Electric Railway in Los Angeles in 1912. Most of these cars were used in Eugene. *Author's collection.*

> *A car crowded to the doors with people who had just come from the ball game in Athletic Park was ready to leave the southern end of the line when the accident happened, putting the system entirely out of commission.*[4]

Electric trains first rolled up to the new OE depot in Albany on the Fourth of July 1912, two months before the OE line was completed to Eugene. Meanwhile, the SP "Red Electric" interurban line reached its southern terminus eleven miles away, in Corvallis, on June 17, 1917. Not wanting its competitors to have an advantage, the OE's last addition, on March 25, 1913, was a branch line between Albany and Corvallis. With that, Albany sat at the center of a web of steam and interurban lines.

This period of frenetic railroad-building gave the city its third depot and further enhanced its reputation as the Hub City. In the meantime, rumors would abound regarding what might happen with the city's antique streetcar line:

> *Rumors of a plan to electrify the street-car line running from the Southern Pacific depot in Albany through the principal business street of the town, and to extend this road, installing a complete street railway in the city have*

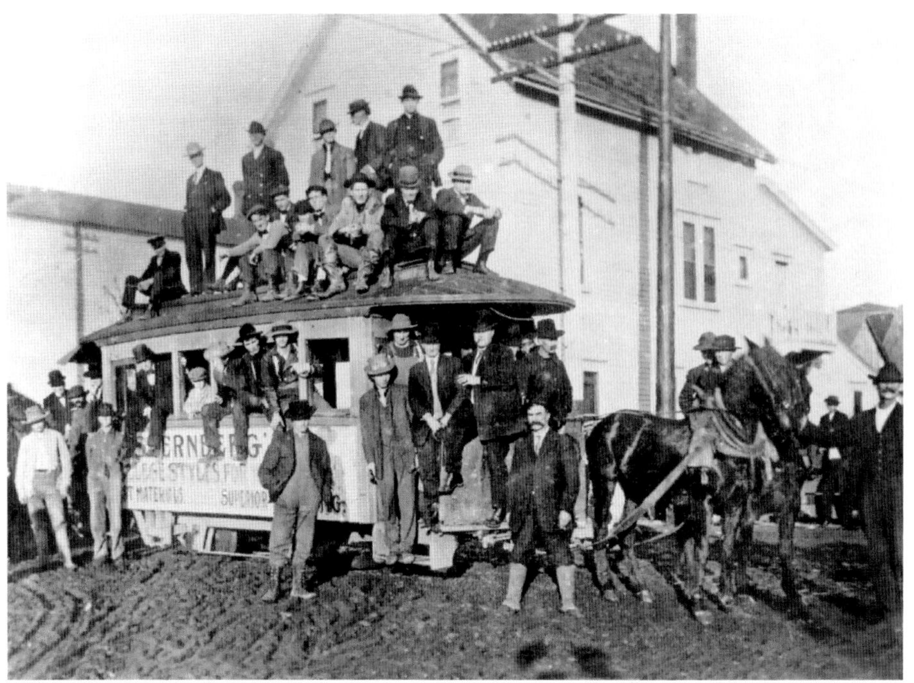

In 1909, a crowd overloaded the streetcar on Second Avenue and Lyon Street to celebrate the last horsecar journey. *Author's collection.*

> *aroused considerable interest in Albany. For years the traveling public have been carried from the railway stations to the business section of Albany in a street-car drawn by horses. Formerly the motive power was a small steam engine, but in later years Albany has been the Oregon town furnishing the spectacle that was seen in the pioneer days of most cities—a car drawn by horses. Numerous times there have been reports of plans to electrify the road, but always the agitation died out.*
>
> *Now, however, representatives of people who have an option on the road have been examining the proposition with a view to putting in a complete street railway system and extending the road from the town westward to the fair grounds, where there will be some good racing in coming years. Also a tract of land west of and connected with the fair grounds will be made into a park, according to present plans, and attractions offered that will make travel on the fair grounds line heavy in the Summer months. The proposed park tract contains a large natural lake, and is an ideal spot for such an enterprise.*
>
> *There is every indication that the car from the Albany depot to the business streets will be operated with electric power within a short time.*[5]

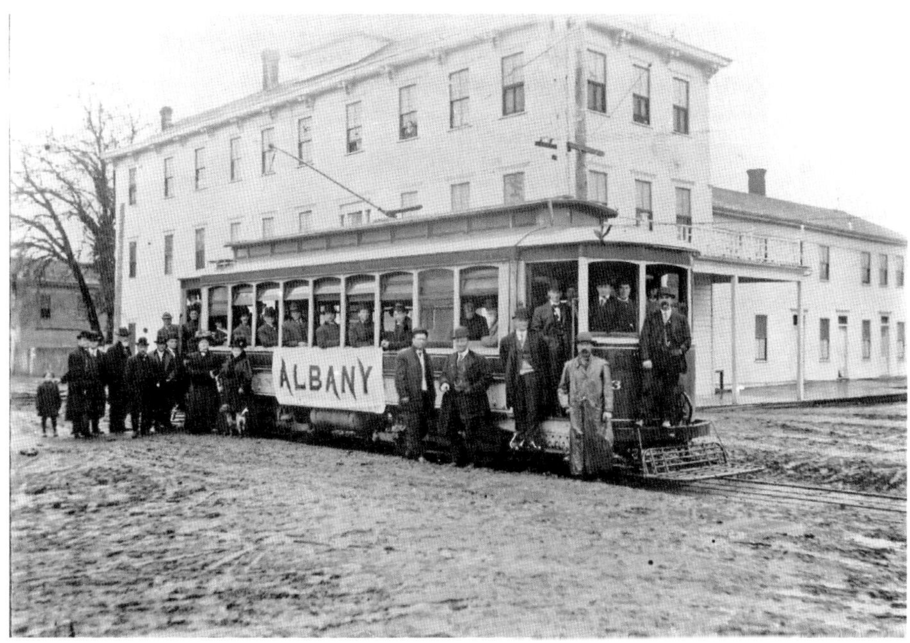

Well-wishers celebrating the maiden voyage of Albany's first electric streetcar in 1909 included dignitaries and members of the press. *Robert Potts Collection.*

In fact, upon purchase of the Albany Street Railway, the PE&E did begin planning for electrification. The upcoming replacement of old-fashioned horsecars with modern trolleys was greatly anticipated, as can be seen in this account in the *Oregonian* looking forward to the city's "Best Year in History":

> *Albany will experience an era of extensive municipal improvement this Summer. More public improvements will be made this year than in any one year in the city's history and from present indications the coming summer will also be a record-breaker for private building, both in the business and residence sections of the city.*
>
> *Chief among Albany's improvements will be an electric street railway system. A. Welch is under $5000 bonds to begin work on a system here before April 11 and the ties have already been delivered for the commencement of work on the Second street line. Work will begin soon and it is said that cars will be running on Second and Sixth streets by this Fall. Mr. Welch has a franchise thoroughly covering the city, having the right to construct passenger lines on Second, Sixth, Calapooia, Madison and Elm streets*

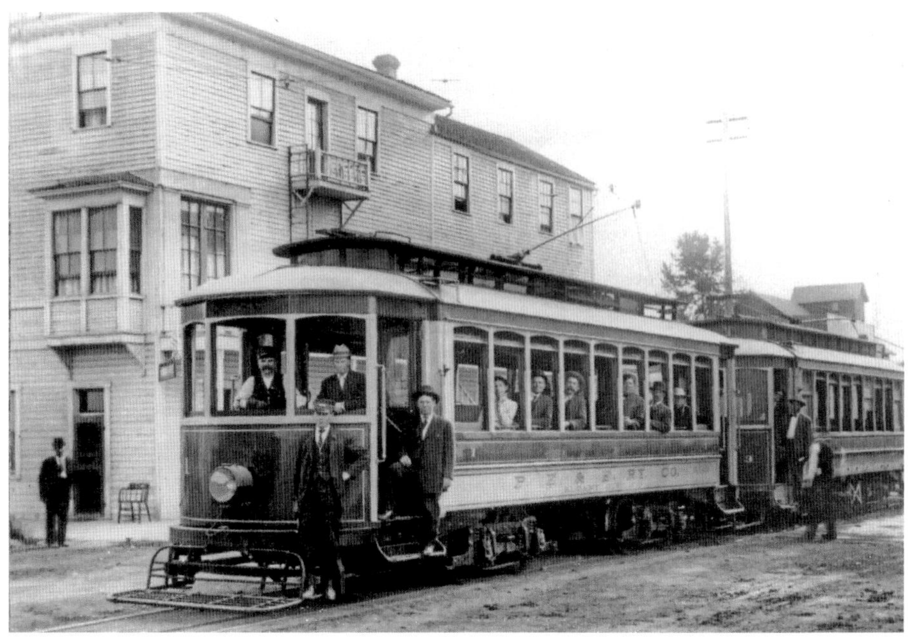

Streetcars Nos. 1 and 3, possibly running together, pose for the camera in front of the Revere House on Southwest First and Ellsworth Streets, circa 1910. *Author's collection.*

> *and a freight line running through the southern part of the city along Ninth street, turning on Ellsworth street to Eleventh street.*
>
> *Coincident with the erection of the street railway system, Albany will have a new union depot for the Southern Pacific and the Corvallis & Eastern Railroad, which is now also under the control of the Harriman interests. The new depot will stand near the present site of the Southern Pacific depot and besides being a union structure for both roads it will stand on the city side of the railroad yards, a change for which the people of this city have begged and fought for for years. The exact plans for the depot have not been made public but Southern Pacific officials have assured local people that the depot will be one of the best in Oregon outside of Portland.*[6]

This prognostication would not prove entirely accurate in regard to the new streetcar route, but the much-anticipated modernization did take place. In the fall of 1909, PE&E held a celebration to commemorate the first trip by an electric streetcar through the streets of Albany. Local newspaper publisher Fred Nutting joined dozens of others to send off car No. 3, which was festooned with a huge banner reading "Albany" (perhaps to differentiate this system from PE&E's Eugene Division). Albany's first motorman, Elba Burnett, was at the controls for the maiden voyage from the terminus in front of the Saint Charles Hotel on W. First and Washington, east on First to Lyon and then south to the terminus half a block from the new Union Depot.

In October 1909, a final half-block extension was made to the Albany streetcar system, allowing trolleys to stop at the south end of the Union Depot. For the next ten years, nine trips were made over this line daily. The fare for the one-mile journey between city center and train station was five cents.

The trolley line was not without accidents, the most infamous of which occurred in 1911 when a marching band musician was seriously injured in an unfortunate mishap with a streetcar:

> *For the loss of his left leg and other injuries, which made him a permanent cripple, Elmer W. Tubbs this afternoon sued the Portland, Eugene & Eastern Railway Company for $75,000 damages. The complaint was filed in the State Circuit Court here by Attorneys Allred S. Bennett and Nicholas J. Sinnott, of The Dalles, and W.R. Bilyeu of Albany, and is the largest damage suit ever filed here.*
>
> *Tubbs was run over by an Albany streetcar, June 20, 1910, and his left leg and both arms were crushed and broken and other injuries suffered. His left leg was amputated above the knee.*
>
> *Tubbs was a cornetist in a band with Arnold's carnival company and the band was parading First street here at the time of the accident. It is alleged in the complaint that the accident was due to the negligence and inexperience of the motorman and also to the fact that the car was not equipped with proper safety appliances. The street was full of people watching the band parade and a great many people witnessed the accident. The plaintiff asserts that he is not only a permanent cripple, because of the loss of his leg and the breaking of both arms, but that the fact that his front teeth were knocked out prevents him from following his occupation as a musician. He has resided here since the accident.*
>
> *The defendant corporation is owned by the Welch Interests and maintains streetcar systems in Albany and Eugene.*[7]

It would appear that the Albany Street Railway was a bit of a barebones operation, one aspect of which was that there was no carbarn in which to store equipment. The former horsecar barn was not used during the PE&E years, so trolleys were simply stored each night on a spur near the train station.

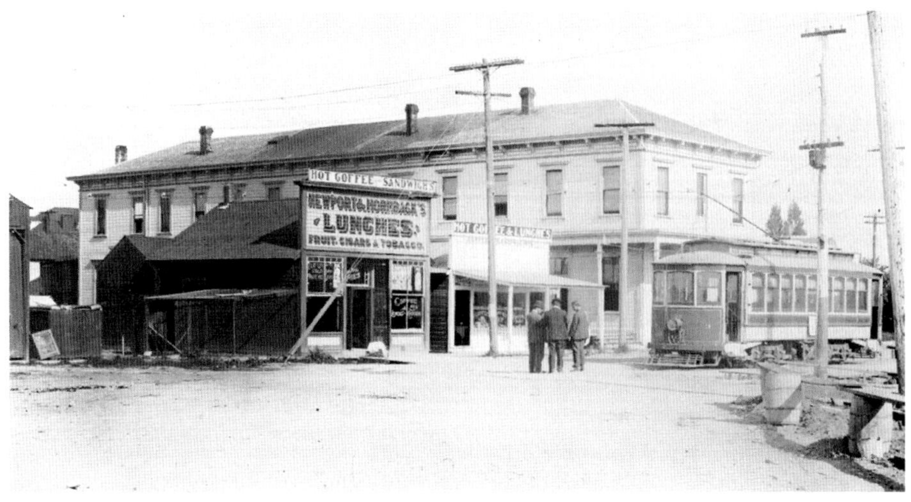

Three businessmen are conferring in the middle of Lyon Street, next to No. 3. In the background are the Newport and Hornback coffee shop and the Depot Hotel. The hotel, once part of the railroad station, was moved here in 1909, when the Southern Pacific Railroad built a new station. A corner of the former carbarn is visible at left. *Courtesy Mark Moore.*

Since maintenance could not be performed locally, Albany's streetcars were rotated with equipment from sister systems in nearby Salem or Eugene, a fact that sometimes aroused local displeasure. Albany residents felt that they were sometimes getting the bad part of the bargain, as can be seen in this 1911 complaint suggesting that the newer rolling stock used previously in Albany was being exchanged for rickety equipment from Eugene:

> *Because the Portland, Eugene & Eastern Railway Company transferred Albany's streetcar to Eugene and sent an old car from Eugene here in its place may ultimately cause the company some trouble over its Albany franchise. A new car, modern of type and well-equipped has been used on the Albany line ever since it was established but this car has now been taken to Eugene and a well-used car, of old design and equipment has been sent from the university city in its stead.*
>
> *The old car has aroused such feeling against the company here that residents of Albany have begun to look up the terms of the company's franchise in Albany and are preparing to insist on strict observance by the company of all the conditions of the franchise.*
>
> *It is said that the terms of the franchise are not followed by the company in regard to air-brakes, fenders and safety appliances. The franchise also provides that the company must construct and operate lines on several*

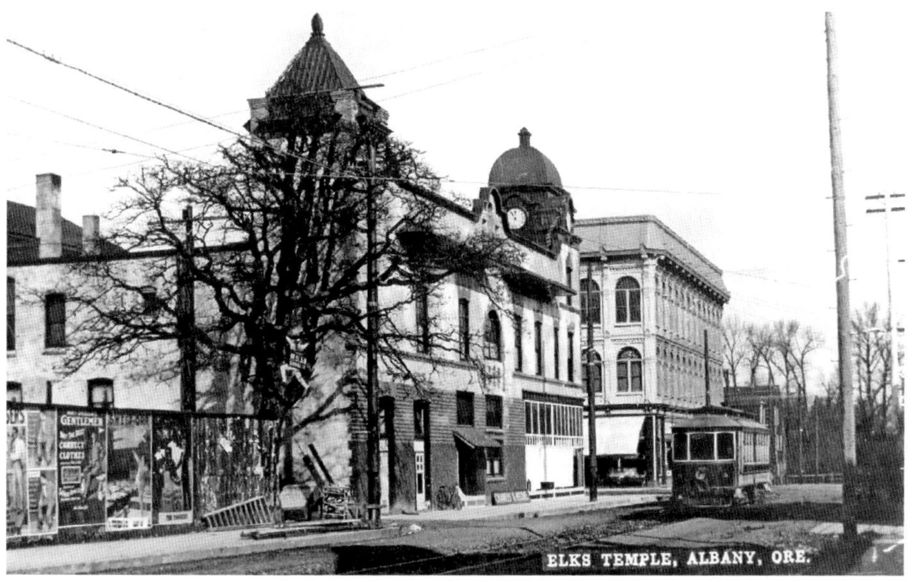

Streetcar No. 3 is passing the ornate Elks Temple on the corner of First and Lyon Streets around 1910. *Robert Potts Collection.*

> *different streets, which now have no lines, by next June to hold its franchise on those thoroughfares.*[8]

The streetcar wars escalated with time. When nothing had changed by 1913, Albany's mayor sent a formal objection to PE&E, requesting that residents be given "better accommodations":

> *Characterizing the streetcar which the Portland. Eugene & Eastern Railway Company operates in Albany as a disgrace to the city, Mayor Gilbert last night requested the ordinance committee of the City Council to consult with City Attorney Swan and prepare an ordinance requiring a new car be placed on the local line.*
>
> *The Council expects to proceed under a clause of the franchise providing for reasonable service. The car now in use here is an old one sent here from Eugene and its appearance is declared a discredit to the city.*[9]

By the time PE&E finally promised to replace the older trolley some Albany residents declared themselves "too proud" to ride their ancient streetcar, inspiring yet another volley from the Albany City Council, which demanded that the car be taken out of service until the replacement arrived:

Ninety-seven residents of First and Lyon streets, along which the Portland Eugene & Eastern operates a lone streetcar, last night petitioned the City council to have the car removed on the grounds that it is "antediluvian" and an eyesore to the neighborhood.

The Council ordered it removed until May 1, when a new car is to take its place. The old car makes so much noise and is out of repair so often, the patrons say, they prefer to walk.[10]

The Albany roster, usually consisting of one or two trolleys, varied because of this rotation. Cars Nos. 1, 2 and 3 were classic double-truck Brill semi-convertibles. This popular design allowed windows to be raised into pockets in the ceiling on warm days, creating a partially open trolley. They were built by the J.G. Brill Company in St. Louis in 1906 and 1907. No. 70 was also a semi-convertible, though a smaller single-truck model (meaning it had four wheels) suited to shorter routes. It was at least comparatively new, being a 1910 product of the Danville Car Company (an Illinois J.G. Brill subsidiary), but its smaller size may have inspired the previous diatribe. Last to arrive in Albany, in 1912, was one of the five "California-style" cars (Nos. 11, 12, 76, 77 and 78) purchased from subsidiary Pacific Electric Railway in Los Angeles. Reminiscent of cable cars in appearance, these trolleys had

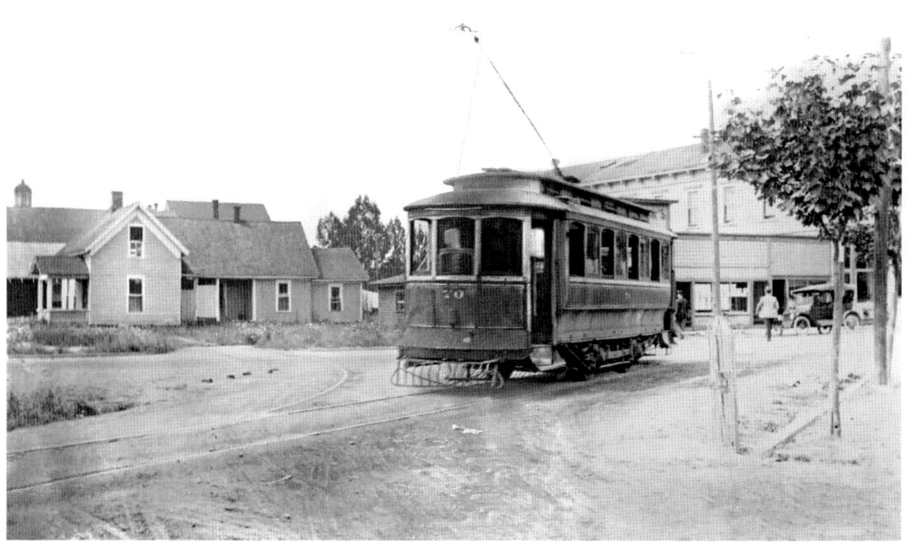

Trolley No. 70 is about to take the dogleg turn on Lyon Street near Tenth Avenue as it departs the train station. *Author's collection.*

originally featured half-open and half-closed bodies. They were not as old as they looked, however, having been built in 1909 by the St. Louis Car Company. They were first transferred to Eugene, where rainy weather may have inspired the closing in of open-car sections.

In the end, business leaders seemed to have held less negative thoughts about streetcars. Just months before the SP brought down the curtain on the Albany streetcar system, a few wondered if the rival OE might consider operating city trolleys on the freight spur that ran adjacent to the Willamette River along Water Street. It was a desperate, if novel, idea that got nowhere: "Local business men are considering asking the Oregon Electric Railway Company to operate a streetcar service on its lines here to connect the east and west ends of the city. The freight and passenger lines connect east and west of the city, so a streetcar would have loop-line service."[11]

The trolley era for one of Oregon's shortest street railways was over in less than a decade. In 1918, Albany became the first Willamette Valley city to abandon its streetcar line. No substitute bus service was provided to the citizens of Albany. This urban amenity, so desirable during the railroad age, may have suffered a tarnished image later on, but what most likely killed it was the SP's unwillingness to continue its funding during the post–World War I recession.

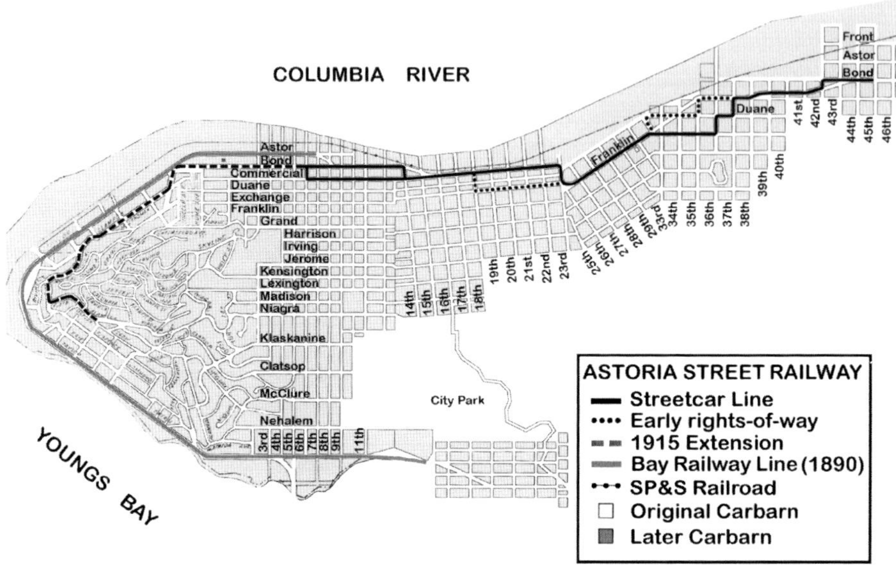

The Astoria Street Railway, and its successors, operated streetcars from 1888 until 1924. This 1910s map shows streetcar tracks and earlier rights-of-way, as well as trackage of the Bay Railway Steam Motor Line. *Map by author.*

Chapter 2

ASTORIA, 1888–1924

As the 1890s dawned, the oldest settlement west of the Rocky Mountains supported a thriving economy. Although Astoria had yet to complete a transcontinental rail connection, competing interests were promoting plans for two electric streetcar lines, two suburban lines, a steam motor line and a cable car system.

The Astoria Street Railway Company began operation of the city's first streetcar line on May 9, 1888, when the first four-wheeled horsecar departed the Oregon Railway & Navigation Company dock on what is now Commercial and Eighteenth Streets. The board of directors included President J.W. Conn, Vice-President W.A. Sherman, Treasurer F.R. Stokes and Secretary F.W. Newell. Superintendent F.W. Newell managed the new system.

Astoria's street railway started with three streetcars, numbered 1, 2 and 3. They were augmented by two open cars, Nos. 5 and 6, which arrived on August 9, 1888. Nos. 4, 7 and 8, were added to the roster on March 28, 1889. This fleet of eight horsecars operated over three miles of track, making fifteen trips each day for a fare of $0.05. All-day passes sold for $1.50.

The idea for a competing cable railway had backing from businessman and sea captain George Flavel, who was one of the richest men in Oregon at the time. The plan was brought before the city council in January 1890:

> *Several members of the city council met this afternoon and considered an application for a franchise for a thirteen-mile cable system to run through*

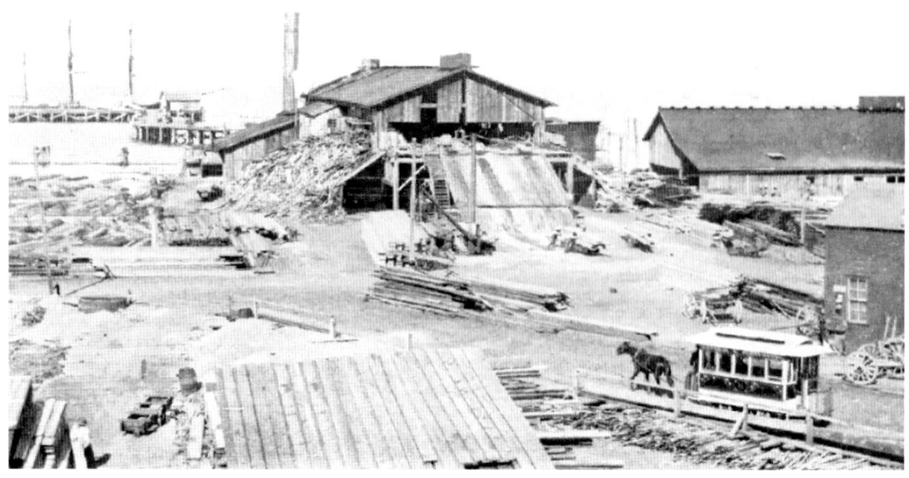

Astoria Street Railway No. 3 is seen next to the Clatsop Sawmill on what would now be Twenty-Fourth and Exchange Streets, during the 1880s. Note the three-masted sailing ship in the background. *Author's collection.*

> *the principal streets of the city. Outside capital is back of the scheme. The company proposes to give bonds to complete the road within two years, but as the city has no authority to take bonds, this would be no security. The only terms that will be accepted by the city council will provide for a certain amount of work within a specified time, or a forfeiture.*[12]

It quickly became apparent that all were not in favor of this ambitious scheme. Within days, the *Astoria Pioneer* came out against the cable railway, arguing that the plan was too important to be rushed into:

> *The city council Tuesday night acted rather too hastily upon the franchise of the cable company, more hastily, in fact, than the circumstances seemed to demand. We are decidedly opposed to so much rush in a matter of importance. It resembles a "railroading" scheme for the members of the council to hastily assemble a few hours before the meeting and fix things so that no delay will ensue when it comes before them for official action.*[13]

The trouble appears to have been that the Pacific Cable Company was only obligated to make a start on construction in order to obtain a franchise, and it could then sit back and wait to see how things developed before continuing with the project. In response, the city council, led by Mayor Crosby, modified the franchise to compel Pacific Cable to build a system that would run from the waterfront, over the Main Street hill, to a suburban terminus:

> *W.H. Dennis, representing the Pacific Cable Construction Company, who has been here for several days negotiating for a bonus of $100,000 for construction of a cable line from the waterfront to a suburban terminus south and southeast, four and one half miles in length, practically closed the deal tonight, and the work of construction will begin within thirty days, with a force of 1000 men. The line will cost half a million and will be built and equipped in the best manner. Dennis left for Portland tonight, and returns Sunday to sign final papers and arrange for starting work Monday. J.M. Thompson, builder of the Portland line, is now in San Francisco, but will return here immediately and take charge of the work.*[14]

In spite of the subsidy of at least $80,000, construction on the Pacific Cable Railway did not proceed. Perhaps principal stockholder J.M. Thompson was distracted by challenges facing his other railway endeavor in Portland. The Portland Cable Railway Company had opened on February 22, 1890, but had been steadily losing money. It turned out that cable railways, which involve complicated engineering, were very expensive to build. At any rate, by the fall of 1890, support for a cable car system in Astoria had fizzled out.

Yet another form of motive power entered the fray on February 13, 1890, when Judge Frank J. Taylor was granted permission to build a steam motor line on streets outside the city limits. His railway would be a beltline, making a circuit around the principal business streets but connecting to new suburbs. Instead of opening the western additions as hoped, the road rounded Smith's Point to terminate south of town on Young's Bay. It should be noted that Judge Frank J. Taylor, president of the Bay Railway Company, had a son and co-incorporator, James Taylor, who was responsible for developing tracts of land along Young's Bay. His franchise was described in the *Oregonian* (modern-day street names have been added):

> *The franchise provides for the construction of a steam motor line from the western limits of the city, entering second street* [Bond Street], *running along that street to West Ninth, thence to Cedar Street* [Exchange Street] *and along Cedar to West Seventh. The conditions of the franchise provide that the road must be in operation as far east as Olney Street by the first of July, and the balance within one year.*

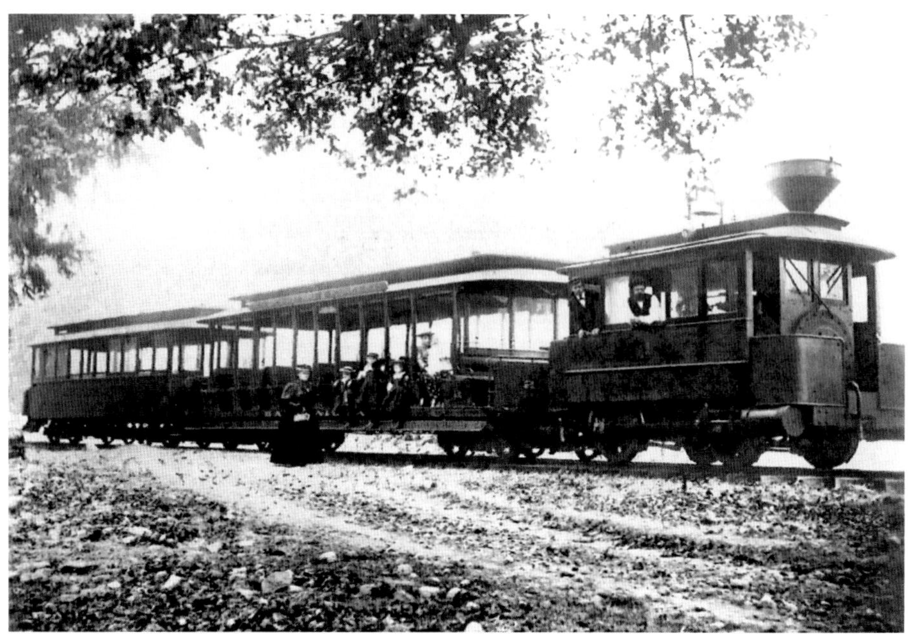

Bay Railway Company steam "dummy" locomotive No. 1, and trailers No. 1 and 2, are waiting at the terminus on Young's Bay circa 1890. *Walter Grande Collection.*

> *If the application is considered favorably, and no doubt it will* [be], *it will be a benefit to the city only second to the Astoria & South Coast railroad. Second street will be opened through the hill, thus giving a thoroughfare to Smith's Point and the western additions, and the same street will be opened through to Olney. Such a road will be to Astoria what the steam motor car system has been to Oakland, Alameda, Berkeley and West Berkeley. These four places are now practically one great city.*
>
> *If the franchise is granted Taylor will immediately organize a company and proceed to construct the line. It will be furnished with the latest Pullman cars with vacuum brakes. The motors have an exhaust chamber and are almost noiseless, while the firebox is so adjusted that coke or anthracite coal makes no smoke. The road will run from West Seventh street around Smith's Point, along Young's Bay, a distance of 3½ miles, and as much further as practicable. The total cost will be about $50,000.*[15]

As construction got underway, progress was reported in the *Oregonian*. On March 12, 1890, "Work is in active progress on the Taylor motor line, which will make a circuit of the city, but will not traverse the business streets.

Surveyors are now locating an extension of this line to reach several suburban tracts."[16] On May 16, 1890, "The track of the Bay Railway Company's motor line has been laid across the lower trestle and is up to the end of a long trestle between the Washington and Seaside canneries. The track will be laid on this in a few days, and by June 1st the whole motor line will be ready for operation."[17]

Track-laying at both ends of the new railway was slightly delayed. Work was held up in town while needed improvements were made to the "roadway" along Water Street (now the Astoria Riverwalk). Like many downtown streets, this was actually a planked road built on pilings over the mud flats. Meanwhile, on May 20, "Little track has been laid on the other end of the road as the company ran out of ties. Completion of the road has thus been delayed. It will not be in operation for about a month."[18]

The June 22, 1890 trial run for the Bay Railway was described in the *Oregonian*:

> *This has been a red letter day for Astoria, marking as it does the advent of the first iron horse, the steam motor of the Bay Railway Company, which made its trial trip, with engineer Arthur Bartholomew at the throttle, and ran around Smith's Point over the completed broad gauge line of this company. Judge F.J. Taylor, president of the company, and chief engineer Thielsen were on board, and J.C. Trullinger, the sawmill king was the first passenger. Another run will be made Tuesday, when a small party of citizens and reporters will take a ride. An excursion is expected tomorrow, and a passenger and Pullman coach is on the way. President Taylor says that if the city council could be induced to fix up a permanent grade for at least four streets running over the hill, there would remain no obstacle to push work on an extension in that direction, and changing it to an electric road.*[19]

The Bay Railway crew also included fifteen-year-old Harry May, who claimed to be the youngest conductor in the United States, if not the world (the other streetcar operation in town, the Astoria Street Railway, started without conductors). The steam motor line he worked for, although well received, got no farther in building an extension "over the hill" than the stillborn cable railway.

Hundreds of curious passengers rode the Bay Railway during a Fourth of July preview, even though its Pullman coaches had not yet arrived. Regular operation commenced on July 7, 1890. As built, the three-and-a-half-mile route ran from a terminus in front of the Astoria Packing Company at West

Seventh and Water Streets (now the Astoria Riverwalk), went west four blocks to the long trestle, turned south at the Washington Cannery and then ran southwest on the planked road that would become Taylor Avenue. The line curved around Smith's Point on Taylor Avenue, turning east onto Olney Avenue at Alameda Avenue, and then continued along the shore of Young's Bay on Olney Avenue, ending at a terminus at Twelfth Street near the shingle mill.

On April 22, 1895, the Bay Railway Company was purchased by the Astoria and Columbia River Railroad (A&C). The A&C was owned by lumberman Andrew B. Hammond, who, with the backing of Southern Pacific Railroad president Collis P. Huntington, built the Hammond Lumber Company and consolidated Astoria's salmon industry under the Columbia River Packer's Association banner. Remembered today as a nineteenth-century "robber baron," Hammond was strongly anti-union, and he became one of the largest private owners of timber in Oregon through means that were not always legal. He was interested in the Bay Railway strictly for its right-of-way, and it is likely that the steam motor line had ceased operation prior to its sale.

The Bay Railway roster consisted of a single 0-4-0 steam locomotive manufactured by the Baldwin Locomotive Works in Philadelphia and two trailers from the Pullman Palace Car Company of Pullman, Illinois. The motive power for Astoria's first mechanized railway was built in May 1890 and featured thirty-five-inch wheels and ten- by fourteen-inch cylinders. It was the type of locomotive known as a steam "dummy" because it was enclosed in a body resembling a streetcar to reduce noise. The trailers included a thirteen-bench open car built in 1888 and a closed car of similar age. The new owners of this rolling stock had little interest in it and did not seek to revive operation.

Even before the Bay Railway started operation, local property owners were lobbying for an electric railway on the opposite side of town. It would have connected with the Astoria Street Railway:

> *A contract was signed yesterday afternoon between the Electric Railway company and Henry Jackson & Co., to begin work which will result in the extension of the present system of the Astoria Street Railway Company.*
>
> *The electric railway is projected from the eastern terminus of the line of the Astoria Street Railway Co. to run around the point down to John Day's* [River] *and thence around Young's Bay to Genevieve street* [Eleventh], *where it will enter the city, running north on that street.*

A branch line will run across to the Seaside.

The preliminary work is to be completed by December 31st, 1889, and the intention is to have the entire work completed, and the cars running by the 1st of next June.

The Sprague system, said to be ten per cent better than competing systems, will be used.

The entire line, as projected, will be about ten miles in length, and will cost, completed, ready for business, about $100,000

The work is in the hands of men who will put it through with all possible dispatch.[20]

Two months later, the electric branch line was seen as imminent:

It is now an assured fact that the electric motor line will be built from the terminus of the present street railroad around Tongue Point and down to John Day river as projected. The cost of the road has been carefully estimated by the gentlemen who are interested in the enterprise, and a corporation will be formed within a few days. The road, which will be about three and one half miles in length, will cost about $25,000, and the electric appliances about as much more. Of the amount necessary to construct the road $34,000 has been subscribed by interested property owners, some upon the condition that the construction commence, and others that the road be completed within nine months, and still others dependent upon the time of running cars. All of these are such as the company can reasonably comply with.[21]

As it happened, no such electric motor line was built. Instead, in September 1891, the Astoria Street Railway Company responded to all the commotion by beginning the process of converting its own lines to electric operation:

Arrangements are in progress to change the present Astoria railway system into an electric street railway. The intention is to begin work as soon as suitable poles can be secured on which to string the wires. A 100 horse-power engine and an 80 horse-power dynamo have been ordered. Just where the power house will be located has not yet been definitely settled, but it is probable that the company's present stables will be the site.[22]

In 1891, a contract for electrifying the Astoria Street Railway was signed with the Thomson-Houston Electric Company of Lynn, Massachusetts.

Thomson-Houston was well known in the Northwest, having built one of Portland's first trolley lines in 1889. The company could trace its roots to the late 1870s, when professors Elihu Thomson and Edwin Houston began experimenting with electric lighting and dynamo designs. In 1892, the company that had become Thomson-Houston would merge with the companies begun by Thomas Edison to form the giant General Electric Company. On November 17, 1891, the conversion was described in the *Daily Astorian*: "The work of changing the Astoria street car motive power from horses to electric goes right on as speedily as possible, and by January 1st, 1892, the Astoria public and all the rest of creation who come this way, can ride in street cars lit and propelled by electricity."[23]

That prediction proved only slightly optimistic. Electric operation actually began on April 30, 1892. A powerhouse fueled by wood from a nearby mill was completed early that year on the planked roadway (now Bond Street) near the east end of the streetcar line, and Thomson-Houston engineers turned their talents to converting Astoria's horsecars into electric trolleys.

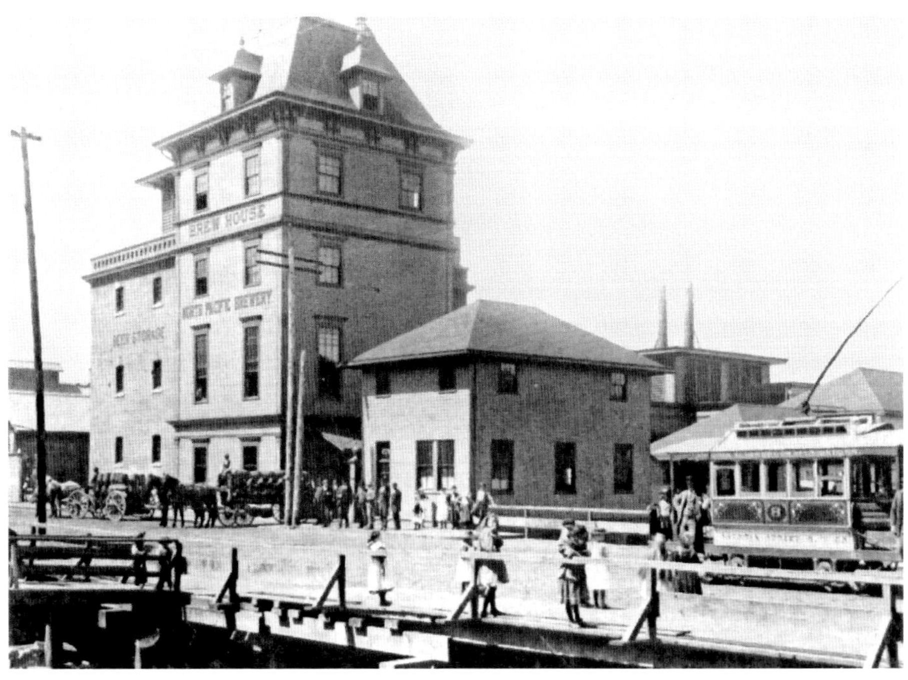

Astoria Street Railway electrified horsecar No. 8 is in front of the North Pacific Brewery on what would now be Marine Drive at Thirtieth Street in this 1890s scene. As indicated on the letter board, this streetcar traveled between "Astoria, Alderbrook and Union Town." *Author's collection.*

Four horsecars manufactured by the Brownell Car Company in 1888 received new Brill trucks equipped with dual fifteen-horsepower motors. Four other former Brownell horsecars continued in use as unpowered trailers. All were housed in the Astoria Street Railway's old carbarn on Hemlock Street (now Marine Drive) between Thirtieth and Thirty-First Streets.

A year after the modernization, Thomson-Houston (soon to become General Electric) bought control of Astoria's street railway. It was common for electric utilities to buy streetcar systems at this time since they would provide power for the street railway and had the capital necessary to improve and expand it. This synergy was at work when the General Electric Company placed options to buy stock in both the Astoria Street Railway Company and the Astoria Gas Light Company in February 1893. A deal was also struck with the West Shore Mills Company, which would be a large consumer of electricity from the new electric power plant. An "Electric Combine" was in the making:

> *The reported bonding of the Astoria street railway by the Thomson-Houston Electric Company is confirmed by the president, who states that an option on the road has been given for a period of 30 days. He would not name the price. The company which has the bond, although identified with the Thomson Houston company, is a separate corporation under the name of the General Electric Company, and has been buying up all the electric plants and franchises it could obtain on the coast. Mr. Conn stated that if it obtained control of the road, Astoria would no doubt see changes, and a complete electric-light plant would be added to the already existing street-car service.*[24]

During the spring of 1893, C.B. Fairchild, editor of the trade magazine *Street Railway Journal*, paid a fortuitous visit to Astoria. His observations provide a good contemporary account of the recently electrified Astoria Street Railway:

> *Although this is a small town of not over 7,000 or 8,000 people, it has an excellent electric line, apparently well managed, and enjoys a liberal patronage. The town itself is built mostly on piles along the river, and the railway, for the most part, is over the water, and extends east and west along the whole front of the city, which is backed by a high bluff, up which it is climbing, however. The cars have twelve foot bodies, and are equipped with two fifteen horsepower Thomson-Houston motors. They are horse cars*

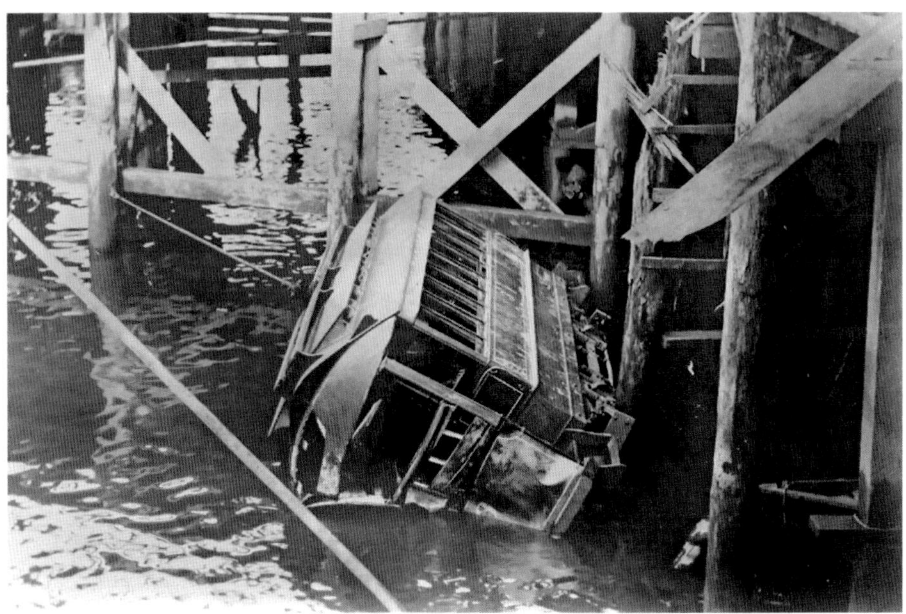

On July 18, 1901, Astoria Street Railway No. 3 derailed after colliding with a hotel bus and fell into the Columbia River. *Walter Grande Collection.*

> *made over, and were originally built by the Brownell Car Company of St. Louis. Fare boxes are provided, and the cars are run without conductors. The power station, which is located near the east end of the line, is equipped with a Russell 125 H.P. engine and an eighty H.P. Thomson-Houston generator, belted direct. Russell boilers are also employed, and the fuel is shavings and slab wood, which is delivered by a rope conveyer from a planning mill about 300 ft. distant. The shavings cost nothing and the slab wood only $1 per cord. The engine room is kept in a very tidy manner, and the generator is made quite ornamental by being painted, the base, spools and fields being of different colors. The engine and flywheel are also painted in bright colors. The line is operated under the supervision of F.W. Newell, who is also one of the principal owners.*[25]

In 1896, General Electric remodeled several Astoria trolleys, extending them from their original twelve-foot length to thirty feet. The process, which began in January and was completed in June, was a major rebuild that may have been accomplished by splicing together smaller cars. In spite of their new length, the rebuilt vehicles continued to ride on four wheels like all Astoria streetcars.

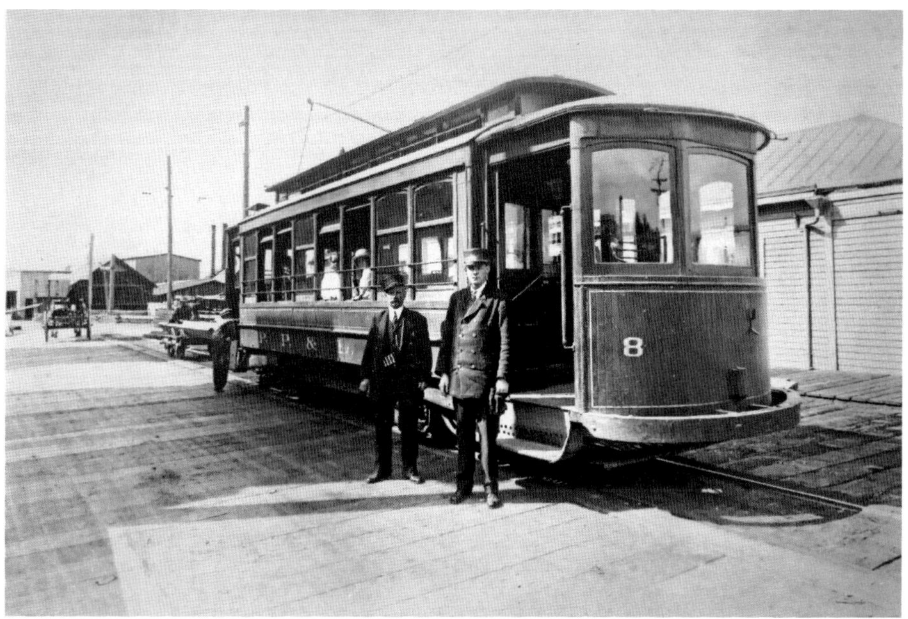

The street planks are clearly visible in this unusual photograph of PP&L semi-convertible car No. 8 towing a flatcar along Franklin Avenue. Motorman Ross Van Osdol (on the right) and conductor Emil Birch are posing for the camera. The Clatsop Mill Company's lumber drying sheds are in the background. *Mitch Mitchum Collection.*

These changes proved costly for the street railway, which, by this time, had expanded to 5.25 miles. In 1899, the overstretched Astoria Street Railway shed a number of financial obligations by filing for bankruptcy. On March 2, 1900—with advice, no doubt, from parent General Electric Company—it was reorganized as the Astoria Electric Railway Company, the transportation division of the Astoria Electric Company.

Seven new streetcars were added to the roster during the Astoria Electric Railway years. Bombay-roofed cars 3, 4 and 5 arrived on December 28, 1901, from an unspecified manufacturer. On February 24, 1903, they were joined by cars 7, 8 and 9 from the American Car Company in St. Louis. These three were equipped with windows that could be tucked into ceiling pockets during hot weather. A trade journal described these semi-convertibles:

> *The last road to receive semi convertible cars was the Astoria Electric Company, although the builders, the American Car Company, made shipment at practically the same time as cars for Eugene, also in Oregon, were ready to go forward. Astoria is a flourishing seaside resort with a*

climate that makes a semi-convertible car particularly desirable for service, especially during the rainy season. At present the system consists of 5 miles of tracks, over which 9 motor cars and 6 trail cars are operated, aside from the three new semi-convertible cars just placed in service.[26]

In 1910, the Astoria Electric Railway became part of Portland-based Pacific Power and Light Company (PP&L), which was in the process of merging several utility companies in Oregon and Washington (see chapter on Milton and Freewater). Like its predecessor, PP&L would provide both power and transportation to the citizens of Astoria.

In 1913, PP&L announced that it would extend its streetcar line to "the eastern limits of Astoria and to the Hammond Lumber Company's mill, provided the city will improve Date Street for a distance of 3000 feet." Although most of the requested street improvements were not made, several blocks of trestle right-of-way dating from the original Alderbrook extension (surveyed in 1890) were removed and the new eastern PP&L terminus realigned to Bond Street at Forty-Fifth Avenue.

The eastern terminus for the electrified Astoria Street Railway had been next to the Astoria Box Company's mill and factory. That facility had been surpassed by the Tongue Point Mill, built by George W. Hume of San Francisco in 1904. Andrew B. Hammond purchased the facility, which included a large planning mill and a box factory, four years later. Nothing can be seen of "the finest mill in the world" today because it burned down in 1922.

The last streetcar extension in Astoria was made in 1915, with a line that ran up the hill on Columbia Avenue to Alameda Avenue and then continued around Smith's Point on Alameda Avenue. The new western terminus on Alameda Avenue was two blocks west of the future Captain Gray School. The historic right-of-way on Taylor Avenue (now Marine Drive) used by the Bay Railway had been decided against when planning this extension, as the portion west of Columbia Avenue had been built on pilings.

PP&L expanded the Astoria streetcar system to its peak of 5.7 miles, which included 5.0 miles of track and a little more than 0.5 mile of sidings and passing tracks. The original car house had been built over a gulch on Hemlock Street (later Franklin Avenue and now part of Marine Drive) between East Sixth and Seventh (later Thirtieth and Thirty-First) Streets. Around 1908, it was replaced by a new carbarn and powerhouse at the other end of town on Astor Street near First.

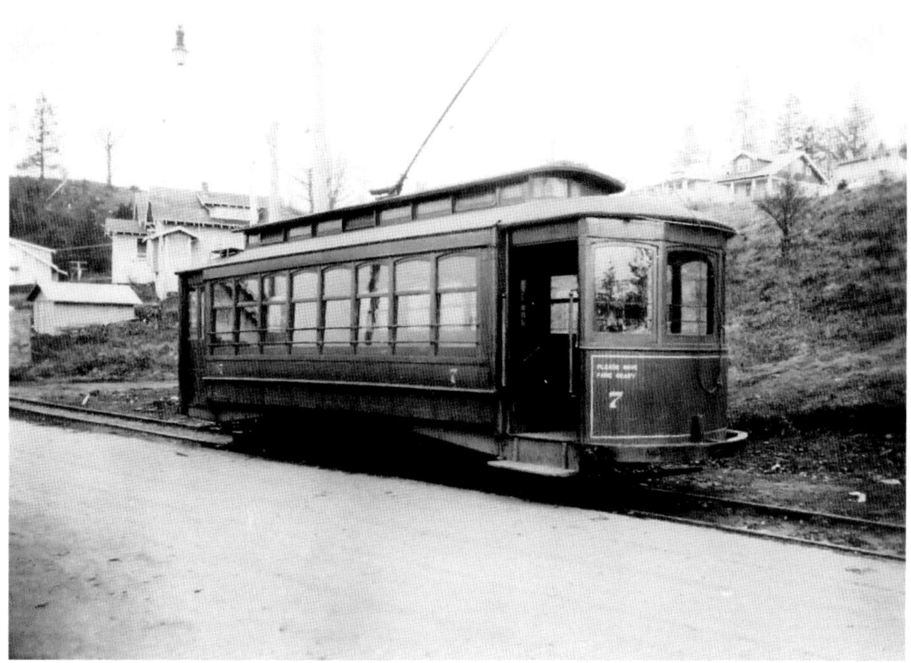

Pacific Power and Light semi-convertible No. 7 is seen at the Alderbrook terminus on February 16, 1921. *Walter Grande Collection.*

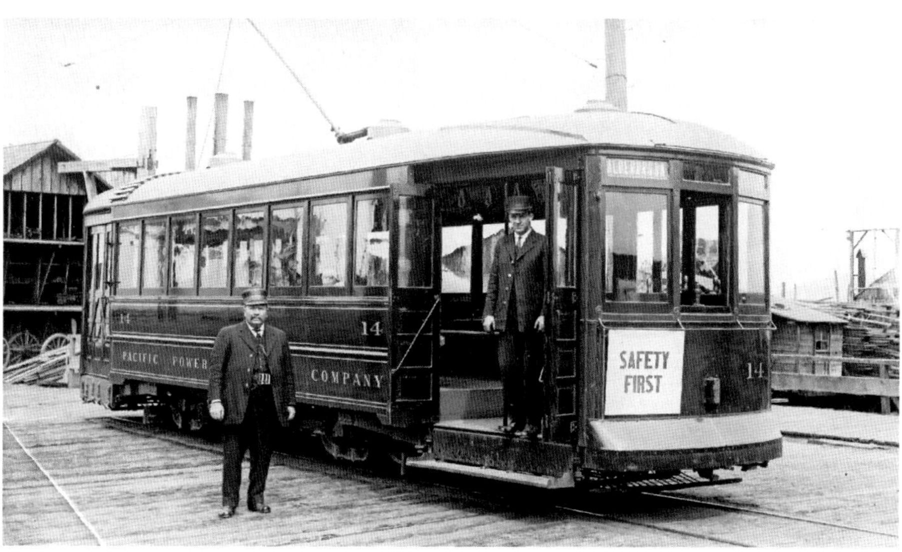

Motorman Eli McConkey (right) and his conductor are in charge of brand-new PP&L No. 14 as it heads past the Clatsop Mill complex toward the Alderbrook terminus. *Mitch Mitchum Collection.*

Astoria's street railway ran through the business district of the city and into two neighborhoods. It was a single-track operation, with passing tracks on Commercial Street. On the loop formed by Sixth, Bond, Fourteenth and Commercial Streets, streetcars ran eastward on Commercial Street and westward on Bond Street. Ten-minute service was provided from 5:45 a.m. to 11:00 p.m. on every day but Sunday and from 7:00 a.m. until 11:00 p.m. on Sundays. In 1922, the fare was increased from $0.05 to $0.07 cents. Discounted tickets were also available; weekly passes were $1.00, a booklet of fifty commutation tickets cost $3.00 and school tickets were forty for $1.75.[27]

PP&L purchased six new streetcars for Astoria, including several of the new Birney Safety Car design, so named because they employed dead man control and automatic doors. Three pre-Birney "Near Side Cars" arrived in the spring of 1913. The next year saw the arrival of a unique Birney car with large PAYE (pay as you enter) vestibules. It was the only car of this type in Astoria. Two regular Birneys followed in 1919 and 1920. All of the new rolling stock was built by Brill subsidiary American Car Company in St. Louis. By this time, the oldest cars had

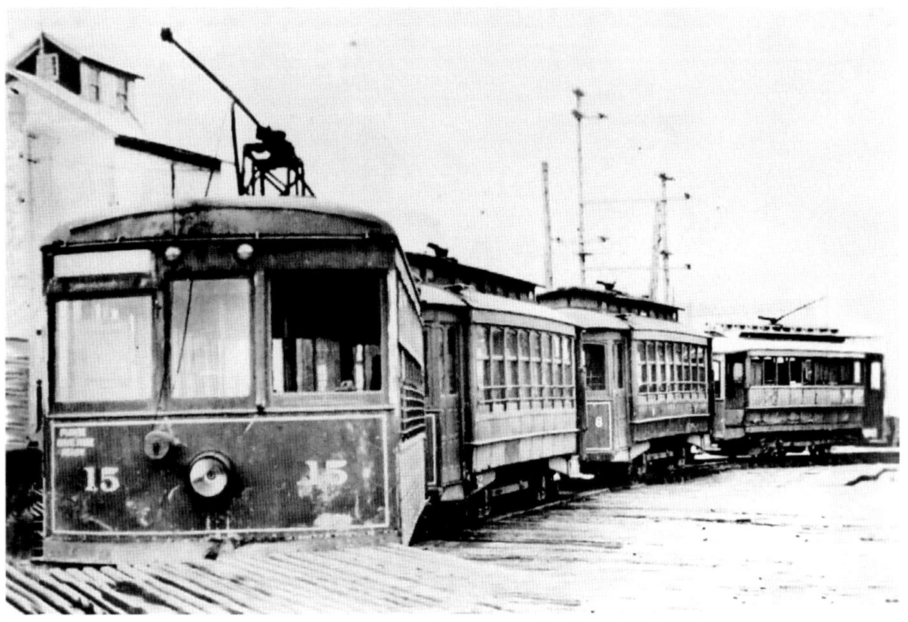

PP&L's streetcars were spared in the 1922 fire, which did not reach the carbarn on Astor Street. The four cars lined up in front of the barn after the fire include Birney No. 15, two semi-convertibles and one of the 1901 vintage veterans. *Author's collection.*

been retired, leaving a roster of eight powered streetcars, one trailer, two freight motors and one service car.

On December 8, 1922, fire destroyed Astoria's central business district, including the plank streets carrying streetcar tracks. The great conflagration broke out just after 2:00 a.m. By nightfall, as reported in the *Oregonian*, it had "swept through 24 blocks of the business district of the city, done damage estimated at $12,000,000, destroyed every department store, hotel, bank and countless small business establishments and taken a toll of two lives."[28] Most sources indicate that the streetcar system struggled on for a few months, operating over the two separated sections. But PP&L soon determined that it would not be cost effective to rebuild. On June 30, 1924, buses of the new Astoria Transit Company replaced the trolleys.

RIVERFRONT TROLLEY

When trolleys made a triumphant return to Astoria after seventy-five years, history seemed to be repeating itself. This time, however, the streetcar line would be a tourist attraction.

Astoria was served by the Spokane, Portland and Seattle Railway (SP&S), which ran along the south bank of the Columbia River, linking Astoria to Portland and eventually extending past Astoria, south along the Pacific coast to Seaside. The railway continued as a freight carrier after passenger service ended in the 1950s. The tracks to Seaside were abandoned in the 1970s, and the line to Portland closed in the 1990s, by which time it had been sold to the Portland and Western Railroad.

The railroad reopened for summer weekend passenger service in 2003. The Lewis and Clark Explorer Train operated between Linnton (just outside Portland) and Astoria, using former British Columbia Rail self-propelled diesel multiple unit (DMU) rail cars manned by Portland and Western crews. Regrettably, low ridership caused the service to be discontinued after two years.

In 1999, the Astoria Riverfront Trolley was born. The heritage streetcar line follows a new route, running along abandoned SP&S tracks from Basin Street to the foot of Thirty-Ninth Street. A new carbarn is located two blocks west of the Basin Street terminal. You could say "what is old is new again," since two blocks of the Astoria Riverfront Trolley line are on a planked-over trestle reminiscent of the old planked

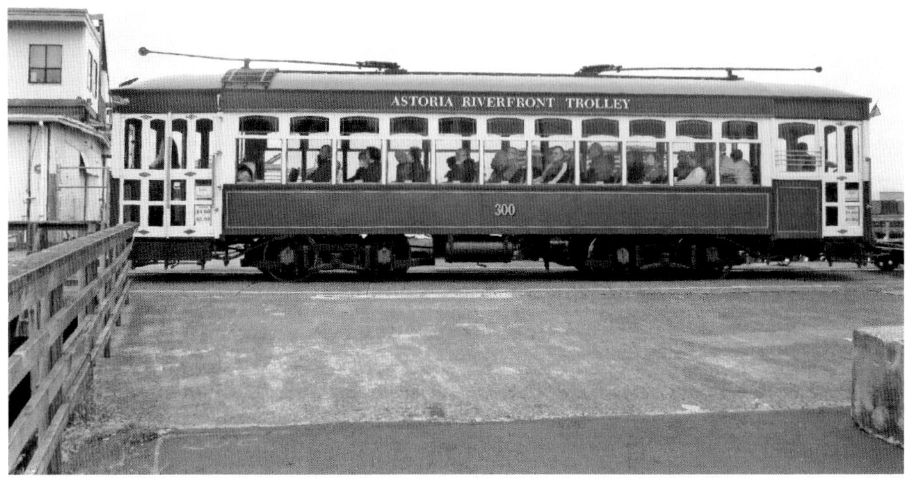

Car No. 300 is seen on the trestle along the Riverfront, traveling in a manner reminiscent of Astoria's earliest streetcars. *Courtesy Mark Kavanagh.*

streets. This section of the new line is shared with pedestrians and motor vehicles.

The streetcar used for the Astoria Riverfront Trolley is authentic but requires a tag-along electric generator to provide electricity since there is no overhead wire. Car No. 300 hails from Texas and is leased for one dollar per year from the San Antonio Museum Association. Like most Astoria trolleys, it was manufactured by the American Car Company. It was one of fourteen cars built in 1913 for the San Antonio Traction Company. Unlike later cars, which featured steel bodies, this trolley is of combined steel and wood construction. The car was donated to the Witte Museum after the San Antonio Public Service Company ceased streetcar service on April 29, 1933.

No. 300 underwent periods of restoration and neglect before coming to Oregon in the 1980s to operate on the Willamette Shore Trolley between Portland and Lake Oswego. For a time, the car was stored at the Oregon Electric Railway Historical Society's original museum site in Glenwood, Oregon.

When the San Antonio car was transferred to Astoria in 1998, it underwent a full restoration. Today's attractive color scheme of dark green and maroon with cream windows and doors replaced the original yellow-and-black livery.

No. 300 runs on Fridays, Saturdays and Sundays from late April through May and daily during spring vacation and over the summer.[29] A ride aboard this volunteer-operated trolley is a great way to experience Astoria transportation as it used to be.

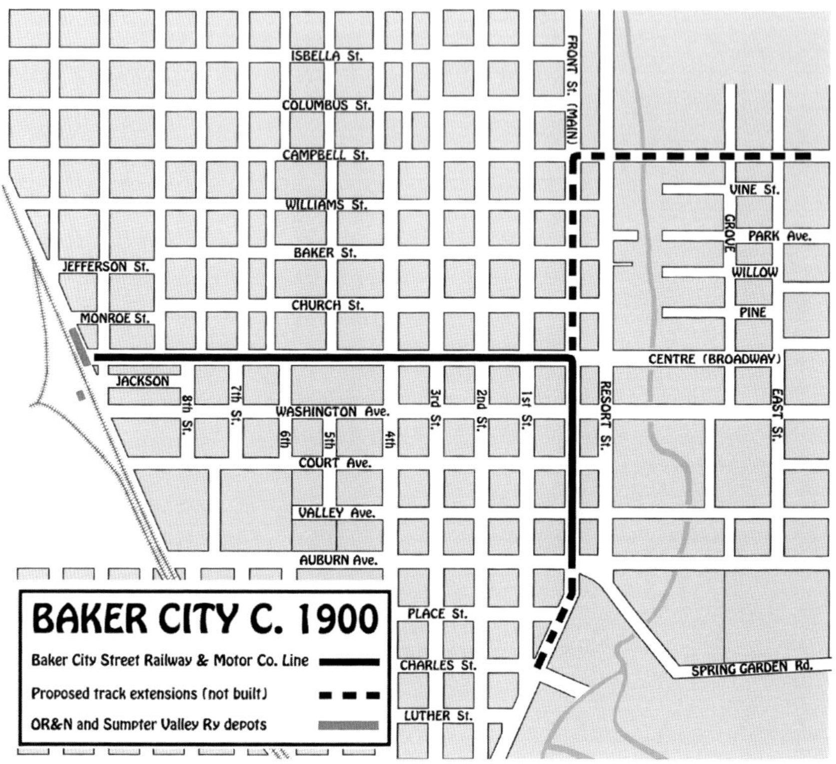

This map shows the Baker City Street Railway, and its proposed extensions, in 1900. The horsecar line ran approximately one mile, from the train station to the Willowvale neighborhood. The carbarn was located at the southern terminus of the line on Main and Auburn Streets. *Map by author.*

Chapter 3

BAKER CITY, 1890–1904

Baker City's first electricity was generated in 1888, the year the streets were surveyed for a street railway franchise. The Baker City Street Railway Company began laying rail on gravel ballast in the middle of the unpaved streets soon after it incorporated on November 8, 1889. Two cars and six horses inaugurated operation on June 4, 1890. The enterprise was headed by John Geiser and his son, Albert. In addition to being railway president, general manager and superintendent, Geiser Sr. was owner of the largest gold mine in the state. The other directors included Henry Rust, E. Silver, H. Dale and T. Calvin Hyde. In total, $50,000 in stock was authorized.[30]

A streetcar right-of-way was also granted, on October 24, 1889, to J.E. Frick of Arlington (a First National Bank vice-president), Oregon; A.P. Campbell, of Denver, Colorado; T.P. Campbell; L.M. Robinson; E.H. Blake; and Samuel White. However, nothing seems to have come of that request.[31] For a decade, the horse-drawn Baker City Street Railway provided unhindered streetcar transportation between the train stations and downtown hotels. Its one-mile line ran on Centre Street (now Broadway) from the Oregon Railway and Navigation and Sumpter Valley Railway depots to Front Street (now Main) and then along Front to Auburn Street. There do not appear to have been any passing tracks. The streetcars were housed in a fine new carbarn and stable near the Main and Auburn terminus. Apparently, the original plan was for the line to continue four blocks southward past Auburn into the Willowvale district, but this extension was never built.[32]

In due time, the railway had difficulty meeting expenses, and Mayor Charles L. Palmer, along with hardware merchant Charles M. Sage, came to the rescue. They would end up leading it through a series of reorganizations, sometimes trading positions as president or vice-president. When their enterprise became the Baker City Street Railway and Motor Company in 1892, it may have involved a merger with the short-lived East Side Street Car and Motor Company. The competing company had been organized two years previously in an unsuccessful attempt to build a line eastward along North (now Campbell) Street to the city limits. "The East Side Street Car and Motor Company has been organized at Baker City, Ore., to build and operate a motor line within the city limits. The capital is $25,000, and the incorporators and directors are J.P. Faull, George Waggoner, P. Basche and J.B. Parker."[33]

According to the 1892 Sanborn fire insurance map, the new streetcar line ran north on Front to North Street and then along North Street to terminate at East Street, where a carbarn was to be erected. It is doubtful that the East Side Street Car and Motor Company ever operated, since Baker City had only one street railway in 1893, and in spite of its new moniker, the Baker City Street Railway and Motor Company was listed as having eight horses and three cars. Two of these were boxcars, and there were no trolleys.[34] Even if the East Side company never turned a wheel, it likely inspired the inclusion of "Motor" in the reorganized Baker Street Railway's new name.

Although the reorganized railway's name may be evidence of the company's intent to eventually convert to steam or electric operation, no such modernization had taken place by 1899. The truth was that Baker City's street railroad never did pay expenses, and some argued that it was simply too short to make money. Sporadic operation now foreshadowed the road's demise. In June, the railway heralded the return of regular service after a lengthy shutdown: "The Baker City Street Railway Company, which has not operated its cars for some time, is putting the track and equipment in shape to begin regular service tomorrow from the heart of the city to the OR & N and Sumpter Valley railroad depots, a distance of 15 blocks."[35] The following March, it had stopped operating again.

As the situation deteriorated, so did the railroad. Deferred maintenance became problematic, and Baker City citizens began petitioning to have the tracks declared a public nuisance. A similar thing would happen years later in Albany, Corvallis and Klamath Falls. By 1902, Baker City's track was in such poor condition that it would have been necessary to rebuild it to continue operation. Surprisingly, Palmer agreed to do so, but only on the condition that the city council grant him permission to build a new electric railway:

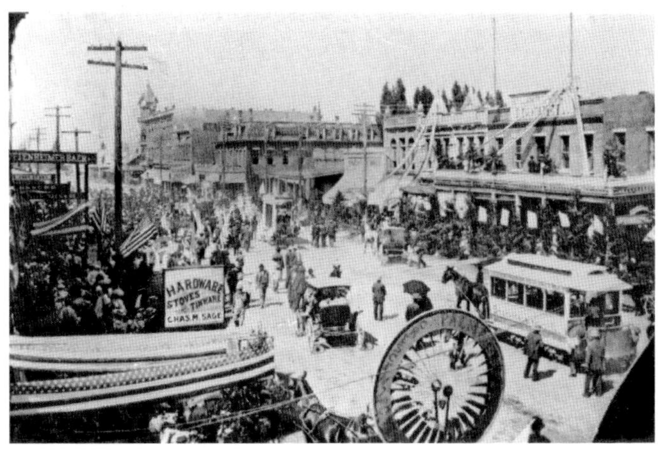

Baker City Street Railway and Motor Company No. 2 is passing in front of the St. Lawrence Hotel on Front Street (present-day Main Street) at Court Street during an early 1890s celebration. In the foreground is a metal sign for Palmer Brothers bicycle repair shop. The building with a tower in the distance is the Geiser Grand Hotel. *Author's collection.*

> *At the regular meeting of the City Council last evening a petition signed by about 75 citizens and taxpayers was presented, asking that the Baker City street-car tracks be declared a nuisance and the company ordered to remove the ties and rail from the streets. Immediately following this petition an ordinance was presented granting a franchise to C.L. Palmer, and others to construct an electric street-car line on any of the streets and alleys not now occupied by another street railway.*
>
> *Mr. Palmer is the principal owner of the old street railway and it is understood that in case the electric railway franchise shall be granted the old line will be converted into an electric road at once. The ordinance for the new franchise provides that at least two miles of road shall be constructed this year.*

Track-laying on the newly incorporated Baker City Electric Street Railway Company never commenced. The new hydroelectric Rock Creek Power Plant then under construction was designed with the capability to provide electricity not only for domestic and commercial use but also for the "new Baker City streetcar line and street lights."[36] However, progress on the dam was slow, as was the sale of stock in the electric railway. When his primary backer bailed out, Palmer was forced to ask the city council for a last-minute reprieve:

> *The City Council has extended the franchise granted to C.L. Palmer for an electric street railroad in this city for a period of eight months. Something over a year ago a franchise was secured by Mr. Palmer for an electric road and a company was organized to build and equip the line. Letson Balliett undertook to float the stock and bonds for the corporation and succeeded in placing a considerable lot of the*

> *stock. Rails and ties were purchased and distributed along the streets, but Mr. Balliett met with financial reverses and the project fell through before the line was constructed. Within the last week a new company has been organized and arrangements made to push the work to completion as soon as Spring opens.*[37]

Palmer thought that he had found a new buyer in July 1904. To be generous, we must assume that Palmer and his business colleagues were taken in by promises of "assured financing" from a new construction enterprise called the Wonder Electric Railway and Improvement Company:

> *WORK ON BAKER CITY ELECTRIC LINE TO BE STARTED AT ONCE. W.G. Drowley, secretary of the Baker City-Oregon Wonder Electric Railway & Improvement Company, who has been East for several months, assisting Major Bonta in his efforts to finance the road, has returned. Mr. Drowley, who is also the attorney, as well as secretary of the corporation, reports that the bonds of the company have been placed in New York and Philadelphia and a sufficient amount of money raised to build and equip the road.*
>
> *Mr. Drowley says that money, while very plentiful back East, is hard to get for investment in Western enterprises just now. This is due to the fact that this is what is termed a "Presidential year," and capital is always shy during a Presidential campaign.*
>
> *Mr. Drowley also reports that a contract has been concluded with a large electrical construction concern for the construction of the road. The work of constructing will begin as soon as the agents of the construction company can go over the proposed line and complete their estimates of the labor and material required to build and equip the road.*

Election year or not, the vague promises made by the Wonder company were not kept. Work restoring Baker City's streetcar line did not "start at once"; in fact, it never got underway. By this time, Palmer would have had difficulty completing the railway within the three-year time frame specified in the new franchise. Now, with no further funding in sight and operation of the old horsecar impossible, Palmer's dreams for an electric streetcar system came to an end.

Amazingly, others now picked up the idea. An electric interurban building craze was playing out across the United States in the opening years of the twentieth century, and eastern Oregon was no exception. New investors came forward with a scheme to restore local streetcar service as part of an interurban railroad that would connect Baker City, Haines and North Powder. The council was willing to grant another franchise and on very generous terms. In April 1907, the city signed an eighty-year agreement with new entrepreneurs:

> *A 80-year franchise was granted by the Council last night to William Pollman and associates of this city to construct and operate an electric street railway also to run an* [inter]*urban line to points outside the city, which will probably be Rock Creek and Haines. The rails and cars are reported to have been ordered and* [the] *work of constructing the tracks is to begin as soon as the necessary implements and material arrive.*[38]

Pollman, a relative newcomer to Baker City, had grown from managing a meat business to become a successful financier and civic leader. His influence in city politics stemmed from positions as president of Pioneer Federal Savings and Loan, president of the Bank of Haines and manager of the Baker Gas and Electric Company. In 1908, he was elected mayor.

Of course, money was required for building something as ambitious as an interurban railway. So, when it appeared that Pollman would get no farther in his quest than his predecessor, investors from Oregon's largest city stepped up. In 1909, Portland capitalists sent one Anthony Mohr to Baker City to arrange for a survey for an electric city streetcar line, as well as an interurban between Baker City and North Powder.[39] The city granted a franchise to the Baker City Interurban Railway, of which Mohr was an officer. Alas, the council was soon once again granting extensions on construction:

> *The City Council has granted to the Baker Interurban Railway a six-months' extension of its franchise in which to begin work on its street railway in Baker City. The company also plans to build an interurban railway from Baker City to North Powder and Rock Creek. Anthony Mohr, Baker City, treasurer and purchasing agent.*[40]

Baker City would go down in history as having Oregon's shortest streetcar line. Its one-mile streetcar line simply proved too short to generate adequate revenue. Still, Charles Palmer exhibited an admirable tenacity in refusing to let go of his dreams for a system that might one day extend to other cities. Of one thing we can be certain: after fourteen years of service, the Baker City Street Railway set a record for having had the longest-lasting horsecar operation in the state.

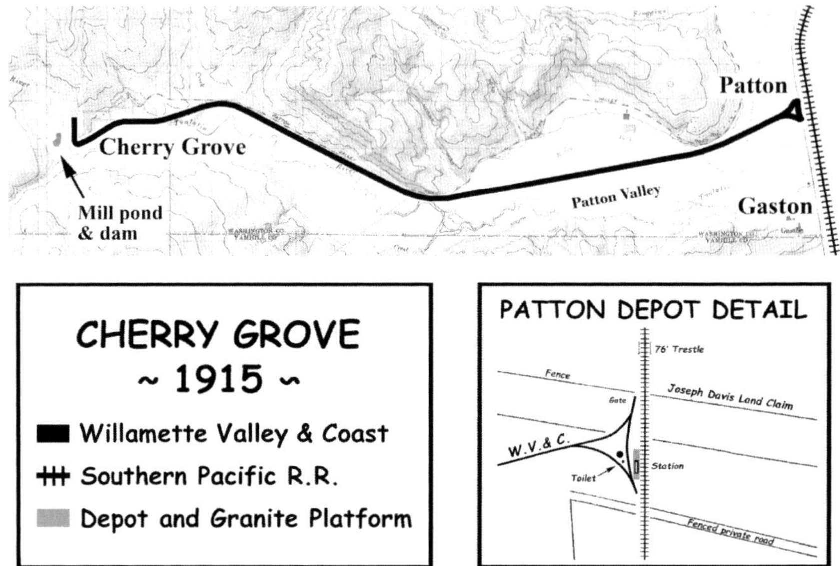

Map of the Willamette Valley and Coast Railway, which operated the first battery-powered streetcar in the West between 1912 and the late 1920s. Tracks to the right are those of the Southern Pacific West Side Branch, where Red Electric trains rolled from 1914 to 1929. *Map by Brian McCamish, modified by the author with permission.*

Chapter 4

CHERRY GROVE, 1912–1933

Oregon's least-known, but most unique, streetcar operation began as a short line railroad. It was the brainchild of lumberman August Lovegren, who had operated a successful shingle mill in Preston, Washington, and owned extensive timberland in Washington County, Oregon. Originally from Sweden, Lovegren arrived in the Patton Valley in 1910 with plans for a new mill and town site. On January 17, 1911, August and sons Phillip and Levi incorporated the Willamette Valley and Coast Railroad (WV&C) to haul wood products from the huge complex, which would include a sawmill and sash and door factories.

The town of Cherry Grove was platted on January 29, 1912, by Levi Lovegren. A post office was established there on May 8, 1912 (it closed on June 30, 1959).[41] The town was named after Cherry Grove of Goodhue County, Minnesota, where August and Hilma Lovegren once resided.

Construction of the new railroad got underway during the summer of 1911. From Patton, the route was as follows:

> *It generally headed west, following straight down the middle of Patton Valley for several miles, then skirted the north end of the valley for the remaining few miles to Cherry Grove. The railroad ran right through town, then continued about ½ mile to the mill and pond. A spur line headed north from the mill, and ran alongside the mill pond and may have been used as a log dump.*[42]

The WV&C got its name in an interesting way. It was actually not the first railroad to be named the Willamette Valley and Coast. The first WV&C was incorporated on August 15, 1867, and after several false starts (and a July 2, 1874 re-incorporation), it was completed from Yaquina City to Corvallis in 1884 (for more information about Colonel Thomas Egenton Hogg and the original WV&C, see the chapter on Albany). Since August Lovegren was a lumberman building a railroad on a tight budget, he may have tried to save money by arranging to take over the name of a defunct line that was still registered as a common carrier. He planned to have service to the Willamette Valley and was only twenty-five miles from Tillamook, so the name fit.[43] In addition to the railroad, Lovegren is thought to have built several logging branches into the foothills west of Cherry Grove.

Construction of the WV&C was completed in September 1911, and regular service commenced on June 30, 1912:

> *Tracks of the Willamette Valley and Coast Railway Company, which has been under construction this Summer by the Lovegren Lumber interests into the Patton Valley section, is now completed and trains will be running in a short time, following which machinery for the large sawmill, which will be built at Cherry Grove, the new townsite, will be shipped in and installed.*
>
> *When the railroad is ready for regular traffic, passenger coaches will be will be added to the equipment of the line., and a regular daily schedule established. Although it is planned to make Cherry Grove an important sawmill center, many other enterprises will be undertaken, including the manufacture of tile and brick.*[44]

There were only a few hundred residents in Cherry Grove at the time, but the WV&C was a common carrier, transporting passengers as well as lumber, agricultural products and mail over the five and a half miles between Cherry Grove and Patton Depot. A passenger and freight station was constructed at the eastern terminus of the WV&C at Patton, which was milepost 753.8 on the SP West Side Branch. "Wye" tracks were installed there to facilitate the turning of trains. An engine house and a depot were also erected at the western terminus of the line in Cherry Grove. The depot was located on the southwest corner of Birch Street.

WV&C ridership may have increased between 1914 and 1929, when the SP Red Electric interurban operated through Patton over the West Side Branch. The first Red Electric trial over the West Side Branch took place between Beaverton and Gaston on January 5, 1914, with regular passenger

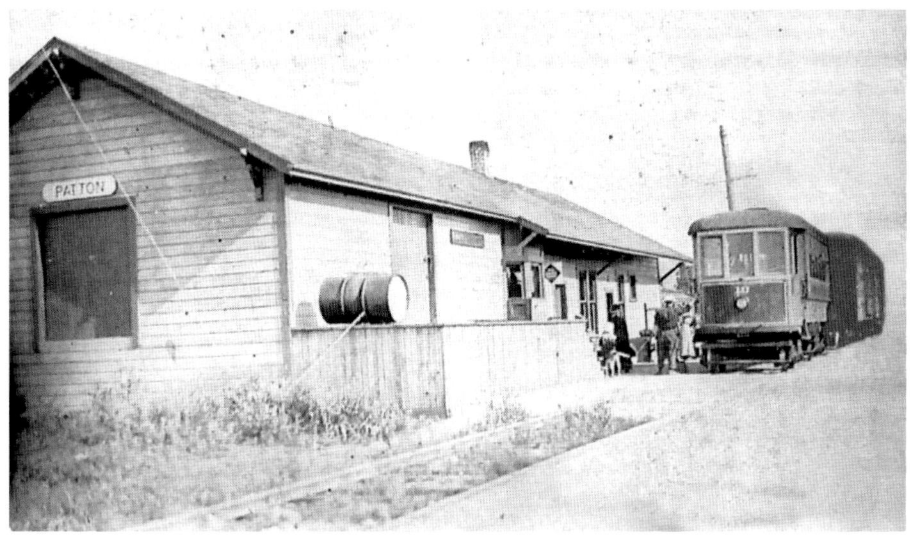

Willamette Valley and Coast Railroad No. 10 is seen at the Patton Depot in this 1910s view looking south from the west side of the station. Oregon's only battery-powered streetcar was manufactured by the Federal Battery Car Company in 1912. *Jane Lyle Collection, Courtesy Kathryn Notson.*

service beginning on January 17. The last Red Electric train ran over this track on July 28, 1929. Longtime Cherry Grove residents remember relatives riding the WV&C and the Red Electric: "The Willamette Valley and Coast RR served this sawmill town until the RR was abandoned, probably due to the depression. My Mother talked about riding a motorized car on the line to Gaston to do shopping."[45] Shoppers could also journey north to Forest Grove.

Although not regularly scheduled service, transportation over the WV&C was first provided by the Lovegren family's Mitchell automobile, which had been fitted with flanged wheels by the blacksmith at the mill. Mitchell automobiles were manufactured in Racine, Wisconsin, by the Mitchell-Lewis Motor Company from 1903 to 1923. Mitchell-Lewis had started as a wagon maker and later branched into motorcycles, but who knew that it also made rail vehicles?

Now comes the most intriguing part of the story. In July 1911, August Lovegren purchased a storage battery streetcar while on a trip back east.[46] This was the first of its kind to be used in the West. In a 1976 interview, Lovegren's daughter, Mabel, remembered this and the other WV&C rail cars:

Transportation was needed. The blacksmith at the mill, Axel Forstrom, only recently come from Sweden, solved that problem with our Mitchell car. He took off the regular wheels and replaced them with flange wheels so that the Mitchell could travel on the tracks. It would hold seven people.

My father had ordered a storage battery electric car from the Thomas Edison plant in New Jersey, and the Mitchell car served the community until the summer of 1912 [sic] *when the electric car arrived. Because of the way the light electric car swayed on the tracks it was nicknamed "The Galloping Goose." The name was soon shortened to "The Goose," and it served the community with twice daily trips until the late twenties, at least, when it was replaced by a gasoline engine vehicle. Some boys quickly sized up the new vehicle and named it "The Skunk."*[47]

It was amazing for this author to learn that this little-known railroad was the only one in Oregon to employ a storage battery streetcar. August Lovegren took a risk when he ordered a vehicle powered by a technology not yet perfected. Although much touted by America's beloved inventor, storage battery streetcars were still quite controversial:

Mr. Edison has been working at the problem of a cheap and efficient storage battery for some twenty years. Some time ago he announced that he had discovered what he was seeking, but it turned out that he had spoken prematurely. Difficulties still remained to be overcome, but he persevered in his researches and the chances are that his success is now complete.

...When the storage battery is perfected, so that it is compact and cheap, its industrial employment will be very extensive. Wherever power is required at a distance from a generating plant it will be available. This includes not only electric cars, but also manufacturing of many sorts and farm work. An economical and not too bulky source of power would be a wonderful boon to farmers. In cities and villages, the storage battery would abate the nuisance of trolley poles and wires. Evidently, therefore, if Mr. Edison's invention comes up to the account, it is an industrial appliance of the highest importance.[48]

August Lovegren, in a single stroke, catapulted tiny Cherry Grove into the vanguard of towns using an important new technology. He invested a large sum of money for the Federal Storage Battery car (an Edison-Beach car exported to New Zealand the same year cost $6,500), but in so doing, he established a streetcar service without having to pay for the "nuisance of trolley poles and wires." His was the only storage battery streetcar in Oregon and the first of its kind in the West.

The news article hints at Edison's overreaching and lack of success with the first rendition of his storage battery. But by 1910, after experimenting for some twenty years, he had worked out most of the kinks in what would be the precursor to today's alkaline batteries. Previously, heavier, less reliable, lead acid batteries were the norm, and streetcars (and other vehicles) powered by them had not been particularly successful. Witness this typical Bostonian skepticism:

> *The fact that a streetcar was successfully run in West Orange, N.J., the other day under the power of Edison's new storage battery means little so far as the fact of operating is concerned. Storage batteries have run street cars before; years ago the experiment was tried here in Boston. But they all passed on into oblivion because they lacked the one great essential.*
>
> *Unless Edison's storage battery can demonstrate that it will run streetcars at less cost than the trolley system requires, taking everything into account, it cannot supplant the older and uglier method. Transportation companies are not conducted on esthetic lines. Economy is the one thing that will appeal to them, if Edison has been lucky enough to hit that necessary qualification.*
>
> *Let us hope he has done it. No greater improvement could now be made in our cities than the abolition of the poles and mazes of wire that now disfigure so many of our streets.*[49]

Mabel Lovegren's memory of the battery streetcar is slightly inaccurate. It was purchased in 1911, and although she thought that it came from the "Thomas Edison plant," WV&C's new vehicle was actually a product of the Federal Storage Battery Car Company (soon renamed the Railway Storage Battery Car Company), which was located in Silver Lake, New Jersey. The railway car manufacturer worked closely with Edison and used his advanced battery technology, but Edison chose not to become directly involved with making the battery streetcars. Instead, he set up a factory to mass-produce batteries: "Thomas Edison started the company solely as a means of selling his storage batteries."[50]

Contemporary sources called this an Edison-Beach car, after co-inventor Ralph W. Beach, who participated in the formation of the Railway Storage Battery Car Company and was behind the design and manufacture of the cars themselves:

Beach began to study electricity, and in 1888 went to work for the Thomson-Houston Electrical Company in St. Paul, Minnesota. By 1892, when Thomson-Houston merged with Edison General Electric to form the General Electric Company, Beach held a position of relative importance, and he became Manager of that company's railway department, which expanded greatly under his direction. It was probably through his activities in that position and his personal interest in electrical experimentation that he became friends with Edison, who addressed his notes to him simply as "Beach."[51]

The general weight, dimensions and speed of a storage battery streetcar can be found in this description of Thomas Edison's 1910 demonstration vehicle:

The car used in the experiment was between seven and eight feet wide and twenty-six feet long, while it weighed only half as much as an ordinary trolley-car. The power was obtained through two motors of a little more than seven-horsepower each, worked by a storage battery. A speed of 20 miles an hour was maintained and it is claimed that the battery needs recharging only at intervals of 150 miles. Stated otherwise, the new storage battery will run a car continuously for seven and one-half hours before its energy is exhausted.[52]

Edison-Beach streetcars were made in both single- and double-truck models. Larger double-truck cars, like the one that became WV&C No. 10, were twenty-eight feet long and weighed nine tons; 190 Edison A6 cells accounted for more than half of their weight. These cars accommodated forty-five people and could attain a speed of thirty-five miles per hour. There were two five-horsepower motors on each truck. It was estimated that the use of fixed axles, with independently driven wheels resting on ball bearings, reduced energy consumption by 25 percent.[53]

The first use of a storage battery streetcar on a steam railroad anywhere in the United States took place during the spring of 1911 on the Long Island Railroad. The WV&C No. 10 was a larger car than that one, but a description still provides evidence of the general operating characteristics of a battery streetcar:

This single-truck car was installed on the Long Island Railroad on April 1, 1911.

To October 1, 1912, it had covered more than 38,000 miles. It makes a schedule speed of 24 miles per hour and because of good tracks and infrequent stops the power consumption is unusually low.

The battery input is 490 watt hours per mile—battery output, 377 watt hours per car mile and 57.1 watt hours per ton mile.

This branch line formerly operated with a locomotive and combination car.

The Beach car makes 72 miles per day, or four trips more than the steam equipment. It has given no trouble—has remained in service with little attention and saves the company about $21.00 per day over the cost of former equipment—a saving equivalent to more than $11,000 in 18 months.[54]

Storage battery streetcars, from a number of manufacturers, saw service throughout the world during the 1910s and 1920s. They were well suited to light service on shorter lines, where expenses precluded installation of regular trolleys. Arduous schedules and steep grades were not the forte of a battery car, but those conditions were not found on the WV&C, where a streetcar could coast down the gentle grade from Cherry Grove to Patton and then return under power. After an operating day, No. 10 would return to the engine house, where it would be connected to a high-voltage DC recharging system—a routine not unlike today's golf carts.

Battery car No. 10 inaugurated scheduled passenger service on June 30, 1912, making two daily 10.8-mile round trips between Cherry Grove and Patton. As noted, the lightweight streetcar provided a swaying ride as it trundled along at a speed of about 20 miles per hour.

By 1915, the WV&C had eight rail vehicles and a steam locomotive. The roster consisted of No. 1, a former Northern Pacific Railroad 4-4-0 "American"-type wood-burning locomotive; a combination passenger and freight coach; a regular passenger coach; battery streetcar No. 10; two boxcars; and three flat cars. Other freight cars were regularly exchanged with the SP and stored on tracks adjacent to the Patton Depot. The coaches were sometimes used in passenger service, but the Edison-Beach car was less expensive to operate and could run on a more frequent schedule since it did not have wait for the creation of a mixed-freight and passenger train. It also did not catch train cars on fire, an event occasionally caused by sparks from the steam locomotive.

The WV&C Railroad experienced a reasonable, if not highly profitable, success, and the town it served was soon thriving. In 1913, a new hotel was in the works, and a large dam was installed on the Tualatin River southwest of town. While primarily used as a log pond for the mill, it was also promoted as a recreational lake:

August Lovengren [sic], *the president of the company, has announced the beginning of a 30 foot dam. It is to be used by the lumber company in*

> *handling its logs and as part of a pleasure resort. Pleasure boats of all kinds will be kept on the lake. A new hotel is to be built overlooking the lake immediately adjacent to the town. A mill of large capacity is to be erected this summer and a brick and tile factory is under consideration.*[55]

Sadly, the dam was to be the town's undoing. In 1914, a freak flood rushed down the Tualatin River, tearing logs from their boom and piling them against the spillway. After a few days of heavy rain, the soil on the south side of the dam wore away. The concrete dam broke on January 4, 1914, causing a flood that damaged the Lovegren Lumber Company mill. An entire season of logs washed down the river. No lives were lost in the disaster, but the mill closed and many people moved away.

In 1915, with the logs gone and the mill idle, August Lovegren sold the mill and railroad to the Haskell-Carpenter Lumber Company. He went on to build a new mill in Washington before passing away in Seattle on February

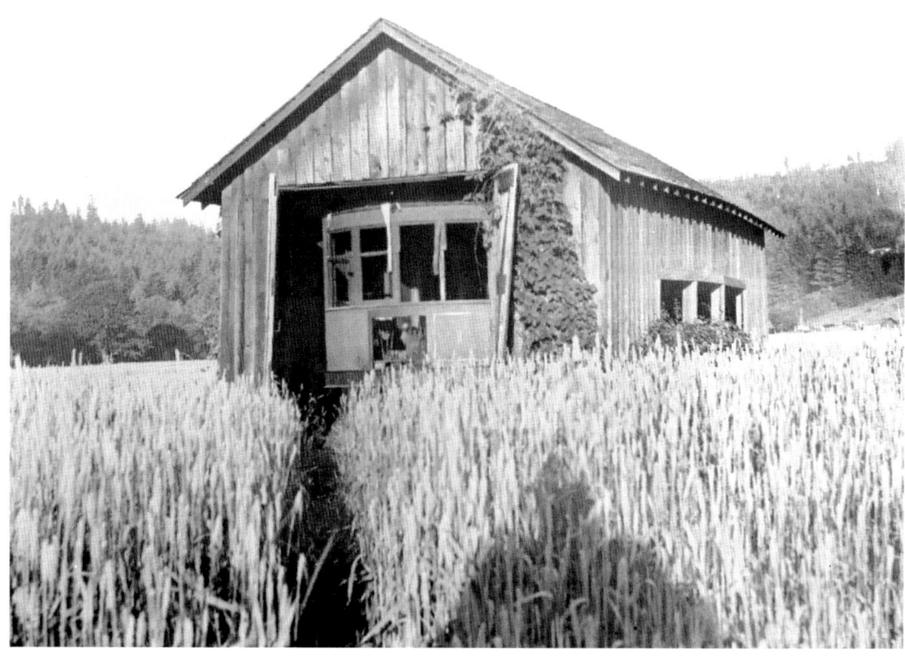

The Willamette Valley and Coast Railroad's last passenger car, the "Skunk," is seen here stored in a wheat field after abandonment in 1935. The large opening on the front was for the radiator of this gasoline rail car. *Courtesy Pacific Northwest Chapter, National Railway Historical Society, John T. Labbe Collection, photo LL-0761.*

28, 1917. The log pond and dam were not rebuilt, but the mill and railroad lived on, at least for a while.

Haskell-Carpenter reopened the mill and resumed operation until going out of business in 1935. In 1928, limited use and no budget for maintenance prompted Haskell-Carpenter to retire the venerable "Goose." Limited passenger service continued until 1933 using a new gasoline rail car, dubbed the "Skunk" by local youth due to the acrid smell of its exhaust.

On July 27, 1935, the WV&C filed with the Oregon Public Utilities Commission for authorization to discontinue all public service on its railroad and take up the rails. It was revealed that no freight or passenger traffic had been carried in either 1934 or 1935, and the government mail contract had been terminated. Permission was granted to abandon the railroad on September 21, 1935.

The "Goose" had apparently been scrapped by this time, and the "Skunk" would soon suffer the same fate. In 1935, after languishing, "propped up on jacks minus any track but roofed over by a shed located in the center of a Cherry Grover's wheat field,"[56] the "Skunk" was sold for junk, and the shed was torn down to make way for more wheat. By the time track removal began in January 1936, the railroad, and one of Oregon's most unique streetcars, was history. When the Alder Creek Lumber Company established a mill at Cherry Grove in 1941, logs were hauled by truck.

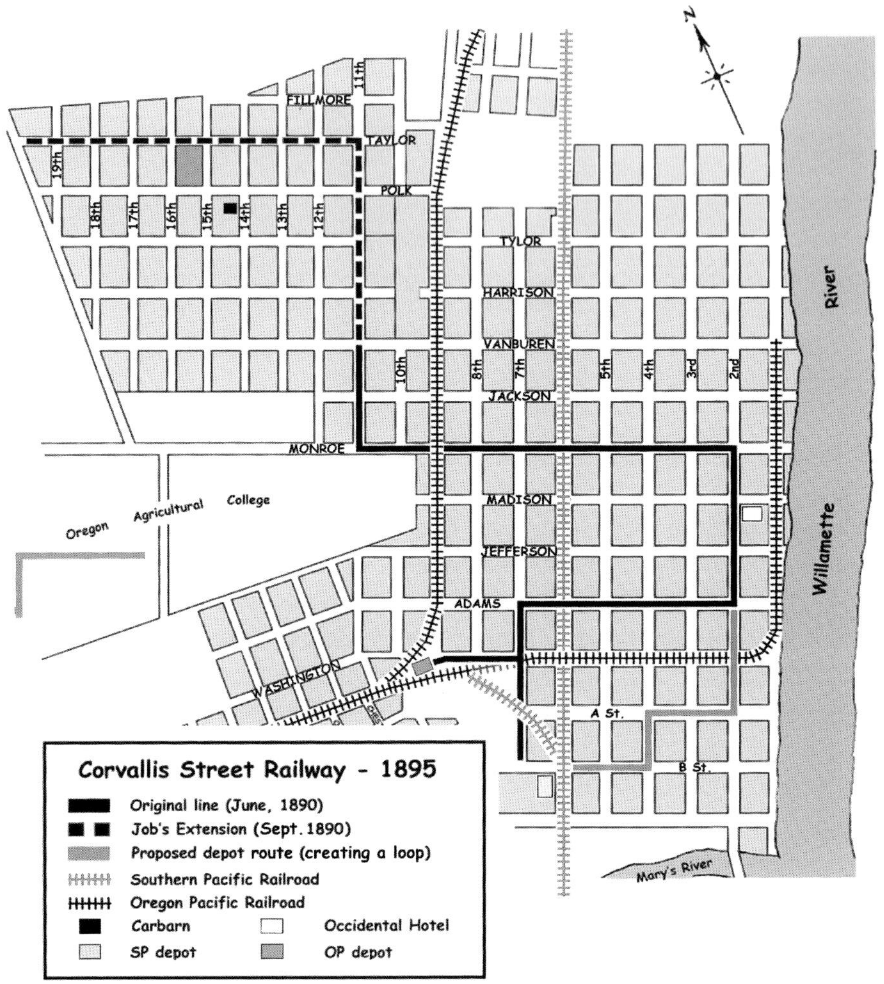

The Corvallis Street Railway operated a horsecar line from the city's two train depots, through the downtown business and hotel district, to Job's Addition between 1890 and 1896. The system had two streetcars and three horses. *Map by author.*

Chapter 5

CORVALLIS, 1890–1896

The Corvallis Street Railway Company was incorporated on December 17, 1889, by a group of real estate promoters led by attorney Joseph H. Wilson and developers Zephin and Beniah Job, as well as Miles Wilkins. On April 3, 1890, the *Morning Oregonian* reported that "[a]ctive work on the street railway will start in about ten days. The contract for lumber, ties and cars was let today."[57] Construction was backed by $50,000 in capital stock.

The horsecar line started service on June 19, 1890, when a streetcar named "Daisy" began carrying passengers between the train stations and downtown hotels. There is some disagreement as to the precise course the streetcars first traveled, however. Researchers have delineated different routes to Corvallis's two train stations. According to National Park Service documentation for the Avery-Helm Neighborhood (through which the street railway eventually operated), "The line began at SW 6th and 'B' Streets, near the railroad depot, and ran east on 'B' Street to 4th Street, north on 4th to 'A' (now Western) Street, east on 'A' to 2nd Street, and north on 2nd to the city limits."[58]

That line would have terminated at the Southern Pacific Railroad depot. But in December 1889, Corvallis citizens had raised a requested $3,000 subsidy to ensure that the streetcar connected with both the SP and Oregon Pacific (OP) depots. In 1897, the OP was reincorporated as the Corvallis and Eastern (C&E) Railroad. In her book *Corvallis in 1900*, Minerva Reynolds noted that the Corvallis Street Railway did, in fact, run to each depot, starting at the SP station and then going to the C&E station:

> *It ran from the Occidental Hotel at Second and Madison, south on Second to Adams, west on Adams to Seventh, from there south to the Southern Pacific Depot, on Seventh and A, then to the C&E Depot at Ninth and Washington. It was later extended up Monroe Street to Job's Addition, making it two and one-fourth miles in length.*[59]

It seems to this author that both accounts are accurate—taken together, they describe a loop, in which outbound streetcars would travel from the SP depot via Washington, Seventh, B, Fourth, A and Second, while inbound cars returned on Second, Adams, Seventh and Washington. A loop, although a digression from the franchise originally agreed on by the city council, would have been far more practical than running from the SP to the C&E station and then unhitching the horse and moving it to the opposite end of the streetcar so as to go back north on Seventh.

Backers of the new street railway formed a syndicate to develop seventy-two acres northwest of the city in a suburb called Job's Addition. Ralston Cox, New York–born manager of the subdivision, joined with Zephin Job and others to lay tracks through their property. Cox had worked in various professions after arriving in Corvallis, including as a barber, grocer and insurance agent. In 1889, he placed ads in the local paper and the *Oregonian* promoting the new addition and the streetcar line. The following advertisement, in the florid style of the time, appeared on Christmas Day:

> *Job's Addition* [is] *the most elegant residence property adjoining the city. Street railways will be running directly through this addition by March 1st next. Prices of lots are sure to double in a short time. Each purchaser of a lot gets a ticket for a drawing of 6 1–10 acre* [plots], *good* [for a] *dwelling, orchard, etc. Maps, description, and price of lots or stocks can be had at Watson, Smith & Co., 4 Stark Street.*[60]

Plans for a branch to Job's Addition were made immediately. On September 12, 1890, the Corvallis Street Railway issued bonds and ordered materials for one mile of road in addition to that already in operation. The extension was to run to Northwest Taylor Avenue and King's Road, more than thirty blocks from downtown. Near the addition, Beniah and Addie Job donated block no. 20 for Franklin Square, the city's first public park. The next year, a car house and stable were erected on Northwest Fourteenth and Polk Streets, near the park. It replaced a previous carbarn at Southwest Sixth and B Streets near the OP depot.[61] Promoters boasted (inaccurately) that Corvallis would soon have more street railway in operation than any other Oregon city except for Portland and Salem.[62]

As completed, the railway would run from the train depot at Ninth Street and Washington to a station on Taylor Avenue near Eighteenth Street. A map published by Ralston Cox shows the line running to a depot close to where the Fred Meyer store is today. The *Corvallis Gazette* noted the "neat waiting room at end of track was furnished with comfortable seats and ice water."[63]

Throughout the 1890s, trade directories listed the Corvallis Street Railway as having two twelve-passenger horsecars and two or three horses. It provided hourly service each day from 7:00 a.m. to 8:00 p.m. for a nickel fare. Students paid a penny, and commutation tickets were available in booklets of fifty. The single-horse streetcars moved at an average speed of six miles per hour and must have operated one at a time over the two miles of track, as there is no evidence of passing tracks.

A second streetcar, and uniforms for the operators, arrived in November 1890: "Ralston Cox, Manager for the Corvallis Street Railway Company, received from San Francisco the new regulation caps to be worn by all drivers and conductors. The style is something like that worn by the OPRR [*sic*]. A new streetcar is to arrive today, [and] it will be put on the line next week."[64]

Ralston Cox painted a rosy picture of the future, predicting that the system would become a motor line, with steam-powered streetcars that would travel at eight miles per hour. There were even plans for a bridge to be built so that a branch could cross the Willamette River into Linn County. Unfortunately, the times were against such improvements, and neither steam nor electric streetcar service would ever be introduced to Corvallis. In the 1890s, Corvallis, like the rest of the country, fell on hard times. Railroads, including the OP, collapsed, and banks failed. President Grover Cleveland called a special session of Congress to deal with the Panic of 1893.

Although Corvallis's railroad era building boom ended in 1893, its unprofitable street railway continued for a time. The Occidental Hotel agreed to underwrite a "hack service" from Second and Monroe to the train stations. The run to Job's Addition was discontinued. The following three-year period is probably when the streetcars were stored at the corner of First and Monroe Streets and the horses kept in a stable in the middle of that block.[65]

All operation on the Corvallis Street Railway ceased in 1896, and the Job's Addition carbarn was pulled down not long afterward. When crews finished removing rails from the streets on February 10, 1900, it was clear that the obsolete horsecars had fallen from grace:

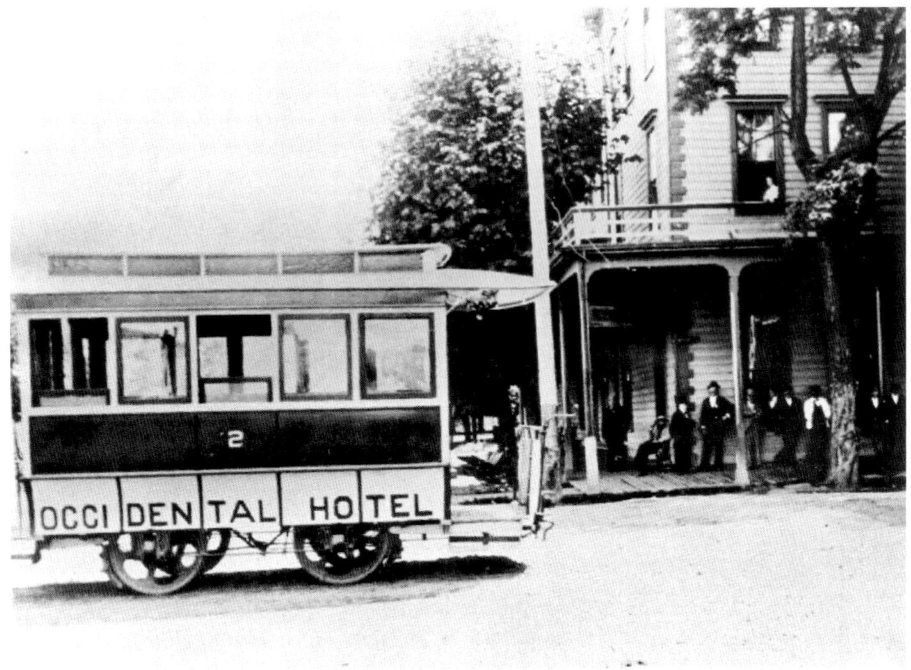

Car No. 2 is waiting in front of the Occidental Hotel on Second and Madison Streets during the mid-1890s, after the Corvallis Street Railway had been shortened to a shuttle service between the train stations and the hotel. *Courtesy Benton County Museum.*

> *The work of tearing up the Corvallis street railway was completed at noon today. The rails were sold to the Oregon Lumber & Pine Company of Viento, Wasco county, for the purpose of building a logging road. The rails will be shipped to Portland on the Ruth Monday morning. This ends the dilapidated reminder of boom times, the Corvallis street railway.*[66]

As with Eugene's first streetcar line, rail from the Corvallis Street Railway found new life when it was removed from city streets and sent elsewhere. Today, a state park near Hood River is named for the former Viento railroad station.

Meanwhile, the desire for a street railway had not been entirely abandoned by Corvallis civic leaders. City records show that the idea of an electric streetcar line surfaced again in April 1912, when an ordinance was passed granting the Portland, Eugene and Eastern Railway (PE&E) "a franchise to construct, maintain and operate a street railroad, together with poles wires and other appurtenances, upon, over and across certain specified public streets in the City of Corvallis."[67]

The PE&E became a subsidiary of the SP, which was in the process of converting several branch lines into an electric railroad network running through the Willamette Valley. The new trolley system was to be built in conjunction with the arrival of its "Red Electric" interurban trains, as described in *Electric Traction* magazine:

> *The utility of an interurban system through the valley appears to have been considered by the late E.H. Harriman and Mr. A. Welch, now of Portland, at about the same time. Mr. Harriman was watching activities of land settlement and community growth along the lines of the Pacific Electric Company at Los Angeles, Cal., while Mr. Welch busied himself in acquiring and constructing city street car systems in the larger cities of the valley.*
>
> *It was determined to expend $12,000,000 in giving the Willamette a complete system of interurban service. The plans contemplated that certain steam roads operated by the Southern Pacific Company should be taken over and electrified, that three new lines should be constructed, the street car systems referred to be enlarged, central stations be provided at Salem and Eugene and that a new street car system be given to Corvallis, all to become a harmonious system.*[68]

Problems arose, however, when completion of the PE&E was delayed. Under the terms of the agreement with the city, failure to complete and operate two miles of street railway within two years would result in revocation of the franchise and an accompanying $5,000 in bonds. As a result, the PE&E was "Ousted from City Streets" on December 24, 1914:

> *The City Council last night revoked the franchises of the Portland, Eugene & Eastern Railway Company for streetcar line rights of way. The bonds of the company, amounting to $5000, were declared forfeited, and the City Attorney was ordered to take immediate action to collect bonds.*
>
> *In April, 1912, franchises for lines of street railway were granted and the railroad company furnished $5000* [in] *bonds, to be forfeited in two years if the company failed to complete and operate two miles of street railway in Corvallis. The railroad at the time was a "Welch" line, and later sold to the Southern Pacific.*[69]

The Red Electric finally reached Corvallis on June 17, 1917, but unlike in Salem, Albany and Eugene, there would be no accompanying street railway. The demise of the horsecar line following the Panic of 1893 had been the death knell for city streetcar service after all.

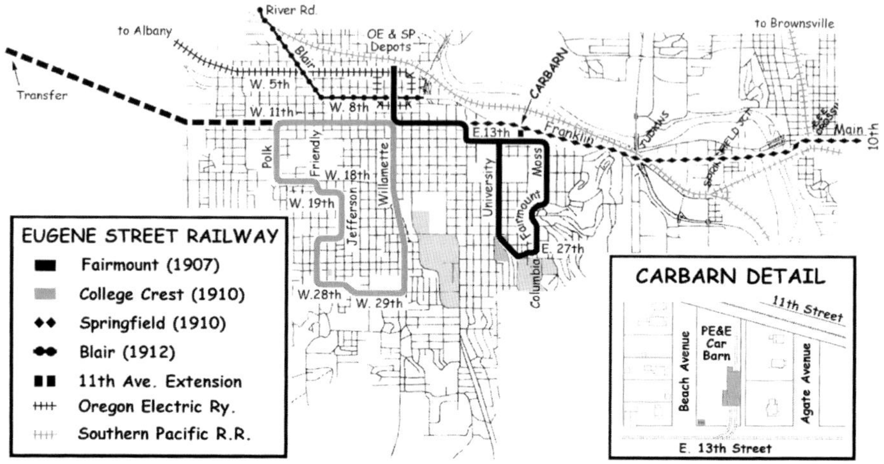

At its peak in 1912, the Eugene Street Railway operated four streetcar lines, including two South Eugene loop lines, a crosstown line that did not share the train depot terminus used by the other lines and a suburban line that connected the cities of Eugene and Springfield. *Map modified from original by Ed Austin and Tom Dill with permission.*

Chapter 6

EUGENE, 1891–1927

On June 26, 1891, Henry Holden's Eugene and College Hill Street Railway began operating a mule-drawn street railway between the Southern Pacific (SP) Railroad depot and the University of Oregon campus. The Texas developer's University Line ran south on Willamette Street and then east out Eleventh Avenue. Two additional lines were planned for College Hill and West Fifth Avenue. As with the Multnomah Street Railway in Portland, streetcars on each line were to have been painted in a different color to allow for easy identification.

Construction on the second line, to College Hill, was completed two days before the inauguration of service on the University Line. Its tracks ran from Fifth Avenue near the SP station, south along Willamette Street, west on Seventeenth Avenue, south on Lincoln Street, west on Twenty-Second Avenue, north on Jefferson Street and west on Twenty-First Avenue as far as Friendly Street. At the end of each line, the seats were reversed, and the mule was unhitched and moved to the other end of the car for the return journey.

Eugene's first streetcars faced challenges during the wet winters. Willamette Street was still unpaved and became very muddy when it rained. In 1936, former car driver Roy Sales recalled people making jokes at the expense of the railway company, sometimes putting out a sign when it rained that read, "Ferry not running."[70]

The College Hill Line was headed toward a proposed trolley park two miles south of town in the vicinity of College Hill near what is now West Nineteenth Avenue. A ridership-generating attraction like this would have been ahead of its time. Oaks Park, Portland's first amusement park, did not open until 1905. But as things turned out, the park was not built, nor was the third proposed streetcar line on West Fifth Avenue.

The Eugene and College Hill Street Railway operated two lines, with approximately three miles of track, four streetcars and as many as ten mules.[71] The cars are said to have been shipped from Chicago, so it is possible that they were manufactured by the Pullman Palace Car Company. Henry Holden's sons, A.G. and Harry, managed the company. Among their employees, Wiley Griffon earned a special place in Oregon history. He apparently accompanied Henry Holden to Eugene to become the only African American streetcar operator in Oregon until modern times. Pauline Walton, a 1904 graduate of the University of Oregon, recalled Wiley and the mule-drawn streetcars in a 1964 newspaper interview:

> *I remember that Wiley used to hitch his mule to a pole near Villard Hall on the campus when he didn't have any passengers on board. Then he would go into the hall to see what was going on. Often, when he came back out, the car would be filled with passengers.*

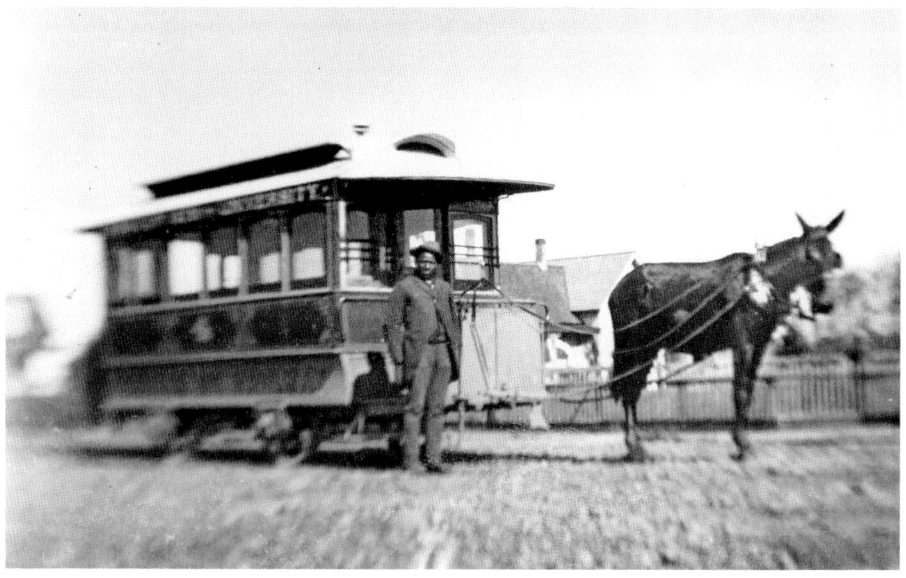

Wiley Griffon poses with mule-drawn streetcar No. 4 in the 1890s, on the line between the train depot and the University of Oregon. Griffon, one of the only African American residents in Eugene, apparently accompanied railway owner Henry Holden from Texas. His pictures are the only ones the author has seen of an African American streetcar operator anywhere in Oregon. *Courtesy Lane County Historical Museum.*

> *There were times when there were so many passengers that the poor mule couldn't get the car started. Then the passengers had to get out and start pushing.*[72]

Even though the Eugene and College Hill Street Railway does not seem to have made money, it managed to struggle along for nine years. It did not cease operation until it was sold to W.B. Dennis in September 1900. The new owner cited a lack of business as the reason for shutting things down.[73] As often happened with abandoned railways, the assets of the Eugene and College Hill Street Railway proved of more value when salvaged for other use. Unused rail was sold to a paper mill in Lebanon, Oregon, in March 1900, while the railway in Eugene was still in operation:

> *The Lebanon Paper Mill Company has purchased a mile of street-car rails, that were obtained years ago for extensions of the street-car system in Eugene. The extensions were never made. The rails will now be put to use in the yards of the paper mill at Lebanon. In addition* [to] *this, negotiations are pending between the same parties for the purchase of the street-car system now in operation here.*[74]

Whether any streetcars went to the Lebanon mill is unknown, but some streetcars are said to have been sold to a Salem company after Dennis took over. In 1903, rail removed from the street was purchased by the Black Butte Mining Company of Cottage Grove, Oregon.

Following a four-year hiatus, a new operator returned streetcars to the Emerald City. The new enterprise was the creation of Alvadore Welch, a multitalented electrical engineer from Portland who was gaining a reputation as a financier, promoter and operator of railways and public utilities throughout the Northwest. Welch was acquiring franchises for a combined interurban and street railway network. His Willamette Valley Company, now called the Eugene and Eastern Railway, became the Portland, Eugene and Eastern Railway (PE&E) in December 1907. Although it never reached Eugene, PE&E's interurban railway would eventually stretch eighty-eight miles south from Portland.

Track-laying for Eugene's new streetcar system began in the summer of 1907, and on September 26, large crowds gathered to watch the Eugene and Eastern Railway Company commence service. Bands played as the first three trolleys, decorated with patriotic red, white and blue streamers, rolled out. Alvadore Welch was on hand to enjoy a ride on

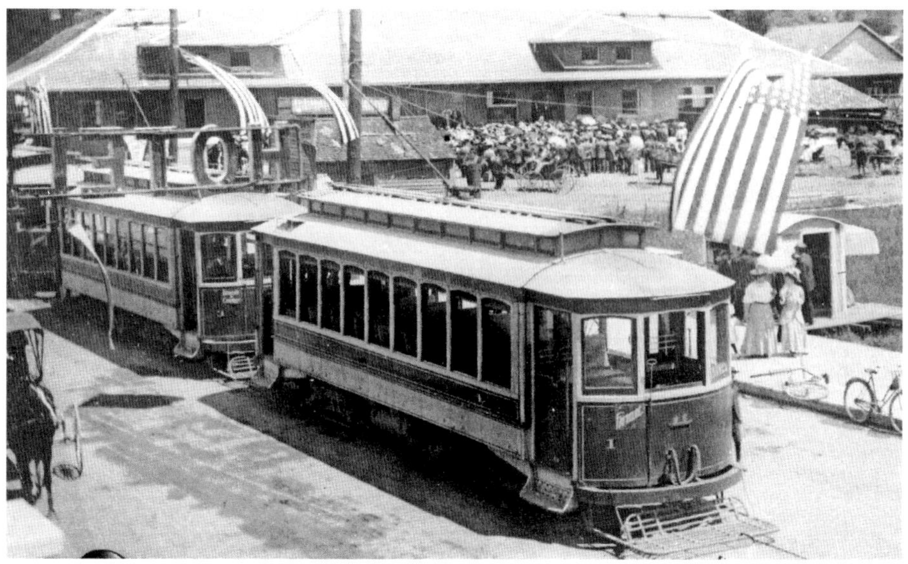

The flags fly as Fairmont Loop No. 1, University and Cemetery No. 3 and a third Eugene streetcar await the crowd celebrating in front of the SP train depot at the head of Willamette Street on the Fourth of July 1910. *Mark Moore Collection.*

the city's first electrically powered streetcars. Initial service ran from the Southern Pacific Railroad station, south along Willamette Street and then east via Thirteenth Avenue, Mill Street and Eleventh Avenue to the University of Oregon campus.

Eugene's streetcars were re-lettered for several different operating companies over the years, but by 1915, after the Southern Pacific Railroad bought PE&E, the Eugene Division was known as the Eugene Street Railway. By this date, the combined city and interurban network that Alvadore Welch had created to challenge the mighty SP had become part of it.

The PE&E would eventually have three city lines and one suburban line, totaling 18.0 miles. All but one of them (the Blair Line) started at the SP depot. First to open, on September 26, 1907, was the Fairmount Line, which served the southeastern part of the city and the University of Oregon. In November, prompted by a $35,000 subsidy from property owners, an extension was added to this line from the eastern edge of the campus on East Thirteenth Avenue to Hendricks Park. The new route was a loop, running south on University Street, onto private right-of-way to the Masonic Cemetery on what is now East Twenty-Fifth Avenue and returning to the U of O via Columbia Boulevard, Fairmount and Moss Streets. The completed Fairmount Line was 5.8 miles in length.

The opening of Eugene's first electric streetcar line inspired a period of construction and development during which civic improvement clubs vied with one another to make their neighborhoods attractive. A 1908 story in the *Oregonian* enthusiastically described this "Best Epoch" in Eugene history:

> *The month of April and the following months of Spring and Summer will mark the greatest epoch in civic improvements that Eugene has known. The activity in building in the residence section is just as noticeable as in the business district and there is no one part of the town to which improvements are confined. Stretching from the easterly line of Fairmount west beyond Blair street and from the Willamette River south to the crest of College Hill, one goes scarcely a block without finding some new building under construction or other improvements being made…*
>
> *Already many of the yards possess great charm and the splendid trees stretching on both sides from one end to the other are the subjects of favorable comment by visitors to the city. One hundred palms have been ordered by the people who live on this street and an Eleventh-Street Improvement Club was organized several months ago for the express purpose of cooperation toward making their street as attractive as possible, but there is also a Civic Improvement Club in the eastern part of town, commonly known as Fairmount, for the East Side Improvement Club, and these people are determined to make their section the most attractive of any, lying as it does between the university proper and the beautiful hill park, recently given to the city by* [the] *Hon. T.G. Hendricks, and known as Hendrick's Park. It is expected that the streetcar line will be completed within a couple of blocks of the park this Summer, affording a continuous line from the Southern Pacific depot to the park. The College Hill Improvement Club, the most recent one to organize for civic improvement, is making rapid strides toward beautifying that very conveniently situated and elevated section of the town known as College Hill. It is hoped to secure a carline for that district sometime next season.*
>
> *Work on the Springfield Extension of the city and suburban streetcar line is progressing satisfactorily and over half the distance from the center of town to the river at Springfield has been graded and several carloads of rails will arrive shortly which, with the ties already on hand, will permit the track-laying work.*[75]

In 1909, an "informal" subsidy by landowners also propelled the creation of Eugene's second trolley line, which would loop through the hills southwest of town. It is interesting to note the role played by out-of-town investors and local property owners in the construction of street railways:

> *Among the substantial improvements for Eugene the coming year will be the construction of five and a half miles of new streetcar line, which will be an extension of the Portland, Eugene & Eastern. The proposed extension will run out South Willamette street, then west around a small hill, then north to Eleventh street and then east on Eleventh, connecting with the fair grounds. This will open a tract of residence property adjacent to the city which, it is assumed, will be improved as soon as the streetcar line is completed. This improvement has been in contemplation for some time and persons interested informally offered the streetcar company a bonus. The greater part of the money required was promised a few days ago and President Story, of the streetcar company, of Portland, J.L. Lambirth, resident manager of the*

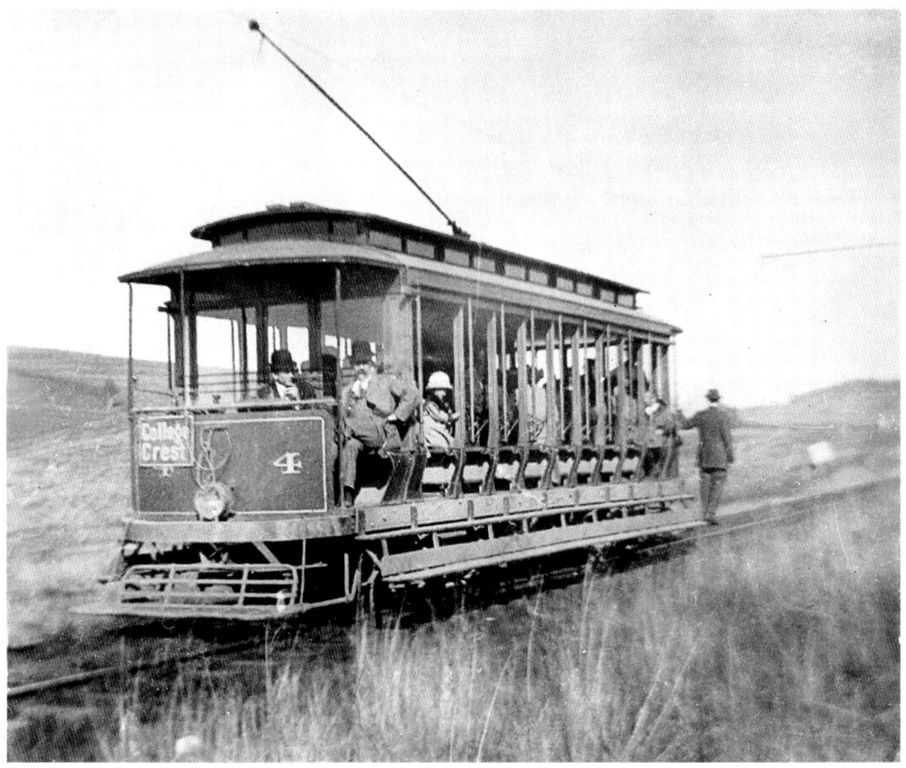

A gentleman is about to alight from open car No. 4 as it traverses the sparsely settled hills on the College Crest Line. The College Crest loop, which opened on July 31, 1910, contributed to the development of southwest Eugene. *Courtesy Lane County Historical Museum.*

> *line's interests here, and Jack Rodman, re-presenting a citizen's committee, spent some time in going over the line and the details of the bonus and contract. A formal contract has been filed with Manager Lambirth and referred to the officers of the company at Portland.*
>
> *The contract calls for the building of five and a half miles of new road, to be completed by August 1, 1910. Construction will afford communication with the southwest part of town.*[76]

Eugene's second streetcar line was completed on July 30, 1910. The 6.2-mile College Crest line served the southwestern part of town and the Fairgrounds. It was another loop route, running along Willamette Street, West Twenty-Ninth Avenue, West Twenty-Eighth, Friendly Street, West Twenty-Fourth Avenue, Jefferson Street, Eighteenth Avenue, Seventeenth Avenue, Polk Street, West Eleventh Avenue and back to Willamette Street.

Although it was not the longest, the next line, the route being built to Springfield, was arguably the most important, as it connected two cities. Springfield residents had been growing impatient while waiting for car service to be established, and in February 1910, two groups approached the PE&E's parent company with a proposal that they install a gasoline-powered "doodle bug" operation between Eugene, Springfield and Coburg:

> *Tired of promises of future streetcar service and seeing a chance for immediate relief, two petitions are being circulated to the Southern Pacific Company, asking that a gasoline car, similar to those in use between Portland and Silverton, be placed on hourly service between Coburg, Springfield, and Eugene.*
>
> *The plan is said to be satisfactory to some 15,000 people along the route. At present it costs 40 cents to ride to Eugene and back, a distance of three miles, or else one can walk three-quarters of a mile to the end of the streetcar line. The service is hourly.*[77]

The Eleventh Avenue Line to Springfield became Eugene's third streetcar line on October 22, 1910. The 4.8-mile run shared tracks with the Fairmount Line to Mill Street and then continued east on Eleventh Avenue and then on what is now Franklin Boulevard, from which it crossed the SP mainline at grade. The route paralleled the SP line as far as Judkins, where it ran onto a trestle and swung east again, toward Springfield. At Glenwood, the line crossed a six-hundred-foot-wide wooden bridge over the Willamette River and then traveled through Springfield on Main Street, terminating at Tenth Street.

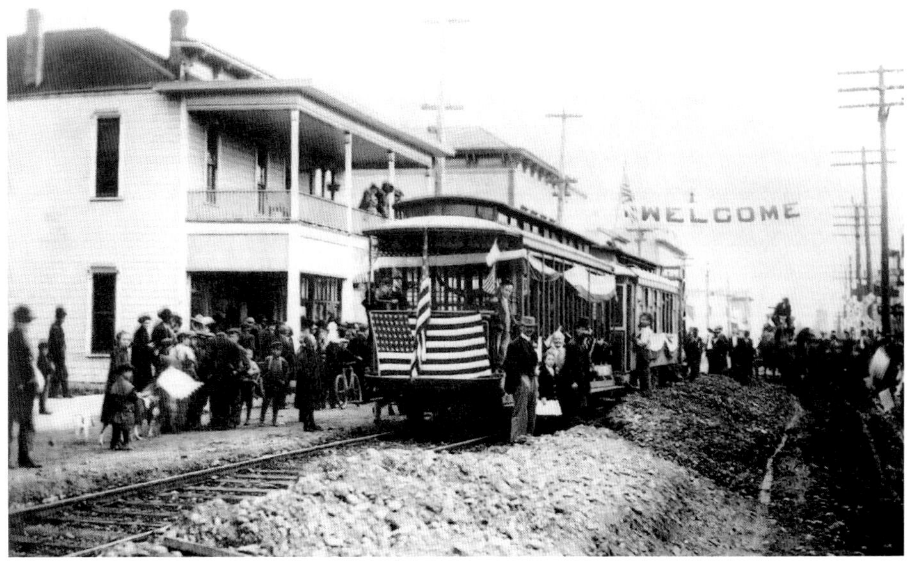

No. 4 and one of the semi-convertible cars are decked out in flags and bunting on opening day for the West Springfield Line, September 22, 1910. The location is Third and Main Streets in Springfield. *Courtesy Lane County Historical Museum.*

Streetcars began running to Springfield two days after completion of the bridge. The *Register* newspaper described the inaugural trip: "Amid the shrieking of mill whistles, [and] the enthusiastic and tremendous cheering of the crowds assembled in Springfield, the first streetcar bearing 125 Eugene boosters rolled across the new bridge this morning, marking a new epoch in the growth of this country."[78]

The Eleventh Street Line was an immediate hit with college students since Eugene was a "dry" town, where drinking alcoholic beverages was prohibited. At midnight on weekends, when the bars in Springfield closed, two-car special trains staffed with sheriff's deputies brought happy passengers back to Eugene. Locals called this the "drunk express."

In 1912, the Eugene end of the Eleventh Street Line was extended out West Eleventh Avenue to a point approximately 1,900 feet beyond Arthur Street, where it turned northwest and connected to the SP's Westside and Coos Bay lines at Transfer. The Eleventh Street Extension was intended to be the Eugene entry point for Red Electric trains from Corvallis.

Had the Red Electrics reached Lane County, they would have terminated at Springfield, where a new depot was planned. Extending the Eugene-Springfield line to make connection with the SP mainline would prove unnecessary, however, because the SP electrification stalled during World War I, never reaching farther south than Corvallis. That did not mean that Eugene was without interurbans, though, because Oregon's longest electric railroad had already beaten the SP to the Emerald City. The Oregon Electric Railway (OE) reached Eugene, 122 miles south of Portland, on October 15, 1912.

Three railroads had been competing for a route through Eugene: the PE&E, the OE (part of the James J. Hill railroad empire) and the Lane County Assett Company, a steam railroad that was organized to build a line from Eugene to Coos Bay via Florence:

> *The three-cornered contest on the part of the Portland, Eugene & Eastern Railway, the Oregon Electric Railway, and the Lane County Assett* [sic] *Company to take possession of Fifth street has stirred up unusual interest here in the development of these three companies.*
>
> *The offer to the City Council of Harrison Allen to put up a bond that the Oregon Electric would be running 33 trains a day into Eugene, within a reasonable length of time, has scattered the doubt as to the coming of the Hill Electric and that the electric line would be extended from Albany to Eugene. People here felt that the probabilities of the Hill people connecting their line with that of Central Oregon, through the McKenzie pass, is quite a possibility. Indications are also strong to the effect that the Lane County Assett Company, which has had two crews of surveyors in the area locating a line from Eugene through the Suislaw* [sic] *pass to Coos Bay are in close touch with the Hill interests.*
>
> *But whether any other electric lines are coming to Eugene or not, this city will have the distinction as soon as the College Hill loop is completed, which will be within ten days, of having more streetcar lines than any place its size in the southwest. The Portland, Eugene & Eastern Railway began its operations here by building a line from the Southern Pacific station to the University of Oregon, after which it built to Springfield. The citizens of the outlying sections of Fairmont raised a bonus for the construction of a loop which connected with the main line at University avenue and Moss avenue. This line now has a 20-minute service. A few of the property owners of Southwest Eugene together with many outside the city limits raised a bonus of $35,000 for which the same company is now constructing the College Hill loop, containing altogether seven miles of track. Just how much more line will be built cannot be known until the Fifth street franchise is given.*
>
> *The Lane County Assett Company has located its permanent line from Eugene, southwest through the Suislaw pass, and surveyors are now at*

work locating the lines which are destined to Coos Bay. This company has also located a line between Eugene and Springfield and has a franchise from the City of Springfield. The plans contemplate a bridge across the Willamette, and this is thought evidence that it expects to go up the McKenzie Valley because the traffic of Springfield for many years will not justify operations of [both] *the Portland Eugene & Eastern and the Lane County Assett Company.*

It is said authoritively [sic] *that the ties have been contracted for, and iron is being purchased for the Fifth Street railway about which there has been such a close contention. The City Council, several months ago, granted a franchise to the Lane County Assett Company over this very important street.*

Everyone here seems anxious to encourage the Oregon Electric to build to Eugene, feeling that it will be the advent of her interests here, which may mean more than simply the extension of the Oregon Electric.[79]

Although a franchise had been awarded to the Assett Company, the Fifth Avenue right-of-way was eventually used by the OE. The railroad to Coos Bay was completed by the SP in 1916, using tracks several blocks to the north.

The Eugene-Springfield Line has been described as having been more suburban than interurban in nature, but a 1922 flood brought unique circumstances to its operation. When the streetcar bridge, and part of the trackage, washed out, the line was rebuilt to share a portion of the right-of-way and bridge with SP steam trains. To ensure safe operation, "staff system" control was installed at Springfield Junction. Under this system, a streetcar could not enter the railroad line until the conductor had taken a metal rod (staff) from a machine that electrically locked signals. Access to the line was closed to any other train until the staff was placed into a similar machine at the opposite end of the line. In addition, streetcars running between Eugene and Springfield were equipped with air whistles to blow at the numerous road crossings.

Eugene's fourth, and final, streetcar line was the two-mile Eighth and Blair Line, which opened in 1912. It ran from East Eighth Avenue and High Street to Blair Boulevard and River Road, traveling over the two streets for which it was named. This was a crosstown route that intersected other lines on Willamette Street. It was the only line that did not have a terminus at the SP depot. Plans for the Eighth and Blair line to be extended across the SP mainline to the community of Santa Clara were never realized.

The original terminus at Fourth Avenue and Willamette Street was replaced by a circle of track next to the SP station, which permitted single-end operation over the two loop lines. This meant that streetcars over those

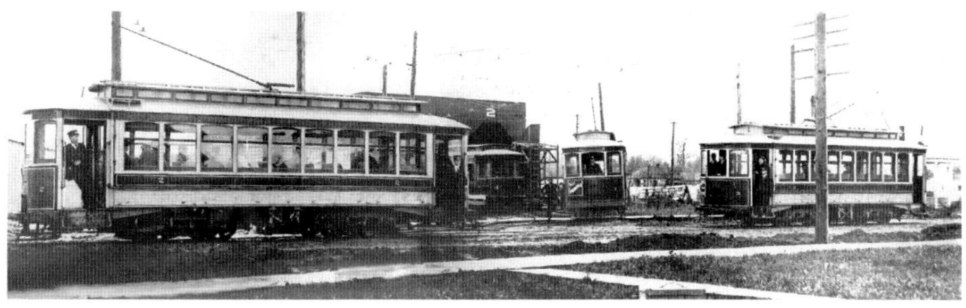

Eugene's rolling stock is well represented in this view taken at the carbarn on East Thirteenth Street around 1910. Carmen and passengers are posing inside streetcars Nos. 2 and 3 on the Fairmount Loop line, while No. 1 sits in front of a line repair car on the ladder tracks and open car No. 4 rests in Bay 2. *Courtesy Lane County Historical Museum.*

lines no longer had to switch ends, change the trolley pole and reverse seat backs at each end of the run. This kind of route, with a circle at each end of the line (sometimes referred to as a "dumbbell"), allowed for one-way travel on the two loops in South Eugene. For example, trolleys on the College Crest Line traveled in a counter-clockwise direction, west on Eleventh Avenue, south on Polk Street, east on Eighteenth, south on Friendly Street, east on Nineteenth Avenue, south on Jefferson Street, west on Twenty-Fourth Avenue, south again on Friendly Street, east on Twenty-Eighth and Twenty-Ninth Avenues and then north on Willamette Street to the double tracks above Eleventh Avenue. Since the other two streetcar lines, Blair and Springfield, did not have loops at each end, they required double-end cars. It should also be noted that while there was double track on the northern end of Eugene's busiest thoroughfare, Willamette Street, most of the streetcar system was single track.

The Eugene Street Railway headquarters, and its first powerhouse, were at East Sixth Avenue and Willamette Street downtown; however, the trolleys were kept in a two-bay carbarn located at East Thirteenth and Beech Streets near the University of Oregon campus. At its peak, a crew of twenty-seven conductors, motormen and shop workers worked here, keeping a fleet of as many as nine streetcars running from 6:00 a.m. until midnight each day. Twenty-minute headways were maintained during peak hours.

The city fare was originally five cents, as in most Oregon cities. The ride to Springfield was ten cents. By the 1920s, the city fare had been raised to ten cents for adults and five cents for youths. An earlier attempt to increase fares was defeated, but the following newspaper account sheds light on how rates differed beyond city limits (much like modern zone fares). Notice also that the proposed standards were based on fares in Portland:

Proposed advanced tariffs on Salem, Eugene and West Linn streetcar lines, to become effective July 1 unless suspended by an order of the Oregon public service commission, were filed here today.

City fares on the three lines involved were increased from 5 to 8 cents. while commutation tickets of 50 rides were advanced in price from $2.50 to $3.65. A feature not heretofore enjoyed by patrons of the lines is the proposed sale under the new tariff of script entitling the purchaser to six rides for 45 cents.

Under the proposed tariff the rate from Eugene to Kincaid, a distance of 2.65 miles, will be increased from 5 to 8 cents, while the rates from Eugene to Midway, West Springfield, and Springfield will be advanced from 10 to 16 cents. Proportionate advances in fares were provided for all intermediate points.

The Salem, Eugene and West Linn streetcar companies, which are owned and controlled by the Southern Pacific company, some time ago filed with the public service commission applications for increases in rates. These applications are pending and no date for the hearing has been set.

The new charges proposed by the companies were approximately the same as those now in effect on the traction lines of the Portland Railway, Light & Power company.[80]

Eugene's first electric streetcars included six double-truck semi-convertibles (No.s 1–3, 8–10) and one open car (No. 4), all built by J.G. Brill subsidiary, American Car Company, in St. Louis during 1906–7. These were rebuilt to closed PAYE (pay as you enter) one-man cars in 1916. In 1912, five 1909-vintage California-style (half open) cars were transferred from the Pacific Electric Railway in Los Angeles, and a longer "suburban" car came from the Twin City Light & Electric Company in Centralia, Washington. The semi-convertibles accommodated thirty-two passengers, the suburban and the California cars forty-eight and the open car seventy-two. The Eugene system was standard gauge and operated with the usual six hundred volts DC.

What would be the system's last car order came in 1914, with the arrival of four experimental, single-ended, semi-convertible trolleys manufactured by the American Car Company. These modern cars had arched roofs, rather than clerestories, and metal underframes. They somewhat resembled the Birney Safety Cars that would soon inundate American cities (see examples of Birneys in the chapters on Astoria and Salem), but unlike most Birneys, they were equipped with two Brill 39-E maximum traction trucks. They

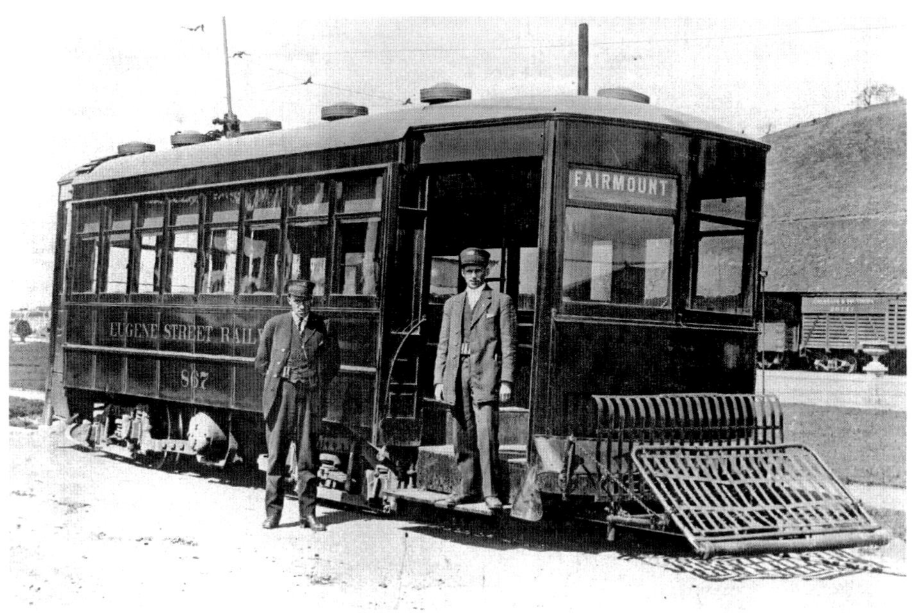

Eugene's last order for streetcars included four like No. 867, seen here next to the Southern Pacific depot, with Skinner Butte and railroad boxcars in the background. These "near side" cars were built by the J.G. Brill subsidiary American Car Company in 1914. *Courtesy Lane County Historical Museum.*

were known as "near side" cars because they were designed for single-end boarding and exiting. Their large PAYE entrances were ideally suited to operation on the two loop lines, and they were easily converted to economical one-man operation in 1915, a move that staved off replacement by buses for another decade. The *Electric Railway Journal* described them as follows:

> *The front platform of each car has a pair of hinged folding doors and folding steps for the regular entrance and exit. An additional emergency exit with folding door and folding step is located in the rear of the car. The seating arrangements, which allow for a total seating capacity of thirty-six persons, include a broad curved seat extending across the rear of the car, six rattan-covered cross seats on each side of the aisle and longitudinal corner seats.*[81]

There had been a few complaints about slow construction of lines in the early years, but few about the streetcars themselves. An exception was the 1910 petition from the University of Oregon faculty asking that the company remove the "flat-wheeled car that runs on east 13th street." But that was a reflection on poor maintenance. Overall, most citizens viewed the trolleys as a mark of progress.

Of course, newspapers printed stories both positive and negative. The latter was true of a 1908 report describing a fatal accident in which a young girl backed into the path of an oncoming trolley. On the other hand, this may well have prompted the PE&E to add safety fenders to its streetcars, since in later years Eugene's streetcars, like those in large cities, were equipped with fenders designed to keep people from falling beneath the wheels:

> *Little Hattie Sumner, the 8-year-old daughter of Warren Sumner of East Fairmount, was run over and killed by an electric car today at the turn in the line at Thirteenth and Alder streets.*
>
> *The child was on her way home from School with some other children and was walking backward. She stepped on the track immediately in front of the car when it was too close to stop. The car struck her in the back and threw her against the front wheels, instantly killing her. Her father was working about a block away on the carline at the time of the accident.*
>
> *The Coroner's jury does not blame the motorman, but censures the company for not having a fender on the car.*[82]

In contrast, a 1916 newspaper story depicted a heroic motorman who dashed from his trolley to retrieve an errant hanky:

> *A woman's handkerchief, dropped on Willamette street in Eugene today, resulted in a suspension of streetcar traffic, while a motorman recovered the bit of linen, which had blown onto the track, and returned it to the owner. The woman thanked him for his courtesy. The car was midway between two street intersections when it came to a sudden stop and the passengers looked from the windows to see the motorman running ahead to pick up the handkerchief. He called to the woman, who had just crossed the street and had reached the sidewalk, attracting her attention and delivering the handkerchief to her at the curb. One of the instructions of the streetcar company is that its employees be courteous in their treatment of the general public.*[83]

As automobiles began to grow in number during the 1920s, the public attitude toward streetcars changed. By mid-decade, those supporting buses over streetcars were in the majority. Editorials in the *Guard* now lamented an unprofitable system that had "never paid dividends" and complained about traffic congestion, unsightly wires and the noisy rumble of streetcars:

> *An open meeting has been called for tonight to discuss the request of the Southern Pacific Company that it be allowed to substitute buses for street cars in the City of Eugene. Some time ago the company removed the street cars on the Springfield line and replaced them with motor vehicles and now it asks permission to do the same with city lines.*
>
> *The advantages of buses over electric rail transportation are apparent to all. Traffic congestion, one of the city's principal problems at this time, would be relieved by removing street cars from Willamette Street. Streets which are now in bad repair due to holes in the pavement next to the car tracks can be mended with some assurance that they will stay in good condition. Unsightly trolley wires will be removed. The radio fan will no longer be bothered by interference caused by passing streetcars.*[84]

On August 19, 1927, the Eugene City Council voted to support the Southern Pacific's request to change the mode of public transportation to buses. As noted earlier, the first line to go was Springfield, which was converted to bus operation in 1926. On September 18, 1927, when the rails were removed from University Street, service on the Fairmount Loop was cut back to East Fifteenth Avenue. The last trolley in Eugene ran on October 15, 1927. With that, the street railway remembered by some as the greatest small-city streetcar system in the United States had come to an end after nearly thirty-six years of operation.

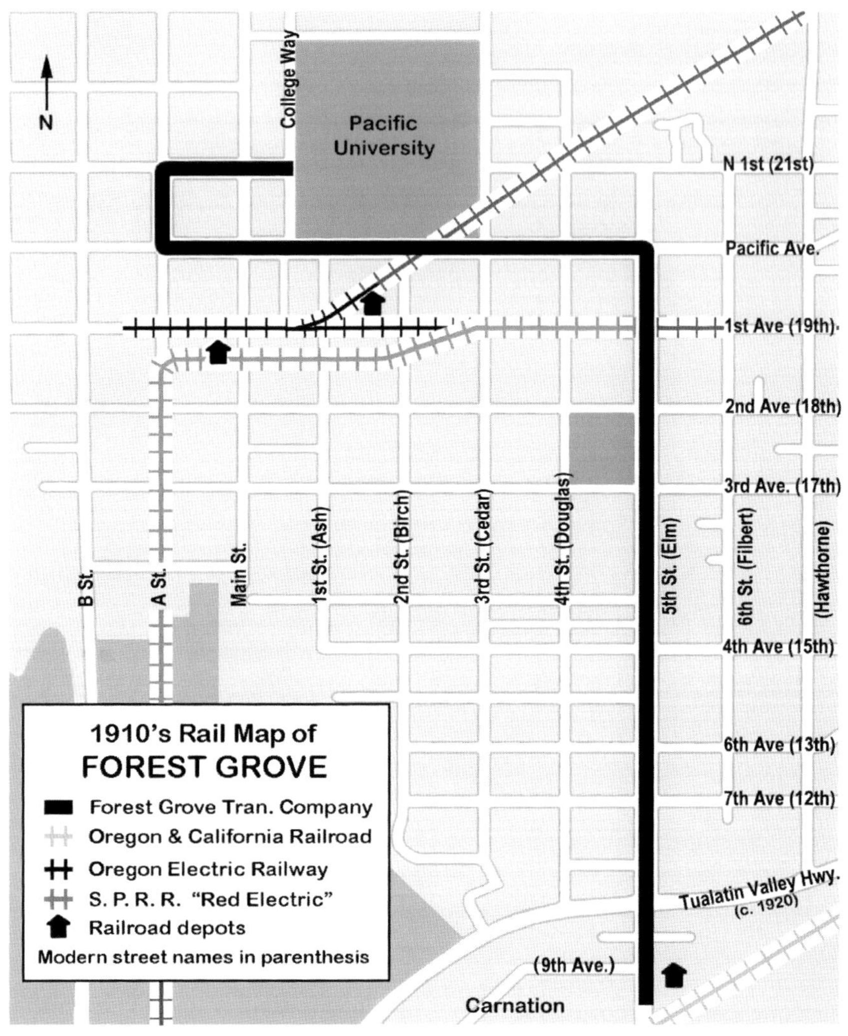

During the 1910s, Forest Grove enjoyed the distinction of being served by two electric railroads in addition to its own nearly two-mile-long street railway. The Forest Grove Transportation Company's streetcar line operated between 1906 and 1911. *Map by author.*

Chapter 7

FOREST GROVE, 1906–1911

In 1906, state senator and banker E.W. Haines led the Forest Grove Transportation Company's efforts to construct a streetcar line between downtown Forest Grove and the train station. In 1872, when the citizens of Forest Grove failed to raise the $30,000 subsidy asked by the Oregon and California Railroad (O&C), the tracks were located a mile south of town, bypassing the city. Haines and his backers felt that a street railway providing transportation between the city center and the railroad depot would be profitable. The January 4, 1919 *Oregon Voter* contained the following portrait of this influential local businessman:

> *As president of the upper house of the legislature in the 1907 session Senator Haines established a tradition for parliamentary ability and effective legislative management. The following year he was elected President of the State Bar Association. He is now a farmer a few miles from Hillsboro. He is one of the few in the House who have been members of four previous legislatures and the only member who is a presiding officer of either body.*
>
> *He was born 50 or 60 years ago, or at least a generation or so ago, in Hardin County, Iowa, coming to Oregon when a boy, being educated in Tualatin Academy and Pacific University in Forest Grove, where later be became a successful merchant, banker and part owner of the local electric light plant. For two years after graduation he taught school.*[85]

The Forest Grove City Council granted Haines's railway a franchise in January 1906, and the 1.7-mile line opened in May 1906. The route ran west on present-day Twenty-First Avenue from College Way to A Street, south on A Street to Pacific Avenue, east to South Elm Street and then south on Elm Street to the Southern Pacific train depot in Carnation near Ninth Avenue.

Financing for the new enterprise was arranged through the Forest Grove National Bank, where Haines served as president. The March 3, 1906 *Electrical Review* described the formation of the railway company:

> *At a meeting of the stockholders of the Forest Grove Transportation Company the following board of directors was elected: Senator E.W. Haines, George G. Hancock, F.A. Watrous, George F. Naylor, J.E. Loomis and Judge W.H. Hollis. The Forest Grove Transportation Company has been capitalized at $10,000, and proposes to build an electric line on the principal business streets from the depot to the business centre of the town. The road is to be in operation by May 1.*[86]

A 1907 railway directory credited the company with a Forest Grove office, repair shops and five cars. The Forest Grove Transportation Company's rolling stock was stored in a barn leased from the Ward Lumber Company. Power for the railway was generated at Lee Falls and rented from the Haines Electric Power Company. Most of this equipment consisted of freight or work cars, including a trailer for hauling mail and packages. Surviving photographic evidence shows only a single large passenger car.[87] The unnumbered standard-gauge interurban is thought to have started its working life as one of two unpowered coaches used by the City and West Portland Park Motor Company, which operated a five-mile steam dummy line south of Portland between 1889 and 1893. After being stored inactive for a time, this car was likely inherited by the Portland Railway, Light and Power Company, which was soon in the process of retiring obsolete equipment.

The Forest Grove Transportation Company's northern terminus was in front of Pacific University on what is now Twenty-First Avenue and College Way. The southern terminal was on South Elm Street adjacent to the O&C station. This was an unincorporated area originally known as South Forest Grove.

The streetcar proceeded over its route at a leisurely pace, sometimes interrupted by derailments, as described in this 1906 account in the *Forest Grove Times*:

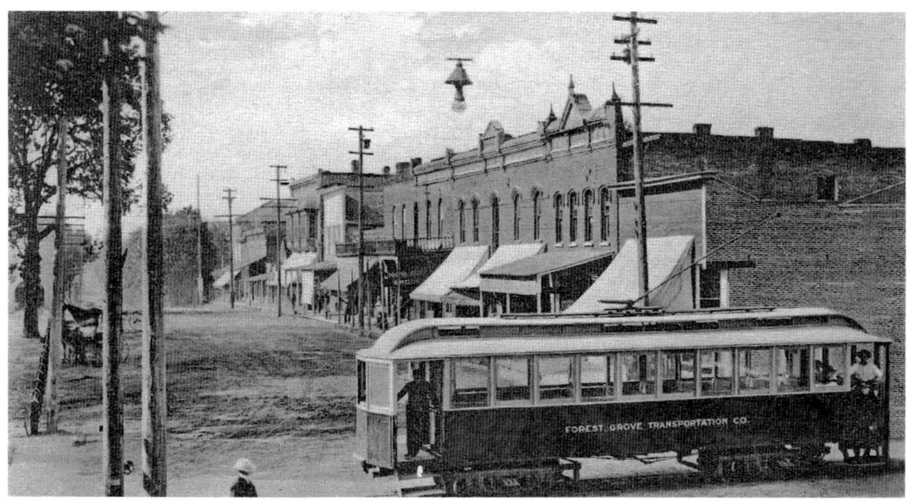

Forest Grove Transportation Company's repurposed interurban streetcar is seen crossing Main Street on Twenty-First Avenue circa 1906. *Postcard courtesy Mary Jo Morelli.*

> *The street car jumped the track just as it was rounding the curve from Pacific Avenue to 5th Street* [now Elm], *as it was going down to meet the noon train last Friday* [August 17] *and the front end started out toward the fence. It was going slowly so it did not go very far until it stopped. It had to be jacked up to get it back on the track, which caused some delay but no damage resulted.*[88]

In 1902, South Forest Grove was renamed Carnation after the Pacific Coast Condensed Milk Company opened a plant there to produce condensed milk. Condensed milk is a shelf-stable canned product in which approximately 60 percent of the water content has been removed. Before the development of modern refrigeration, milk could only be kept fresh for a short time, so condensed milk became very popular. Pacific Coast was an important railroad customer, shipping carloads of Carnation Cream from this location until the factory closed in 1929. A hotel, post office and store were built in Carnation as the population around the factory grew.

Ironically, the streetcar service linking the Carnation depot with Forest Grove became less tenable with the arrival of two new railroads. In 1908, the Oregon Electric Railway (OE) came to Forest Grove, and in 1912, the Southern Pacific Railroad (which acquired the O&C in 1887) began construction of the Red Electric system. This time, franchise agreements saw to it that depots were built in downtown Forest Grove. Before long,

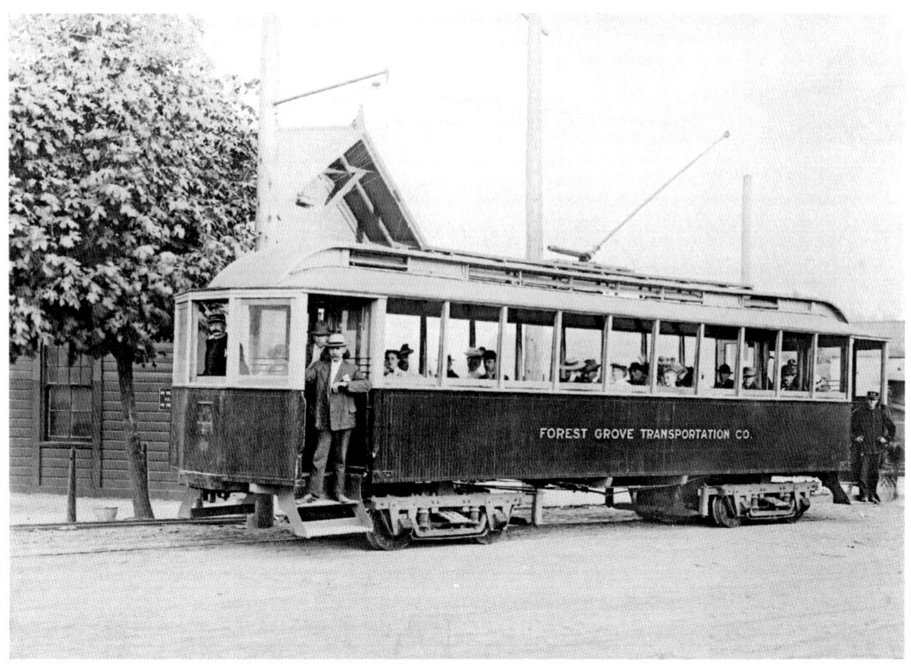

Forest Grove's well-loaded streetcar is seen on Elm Street in front of the Southern Pacific Railroad's Carnation depot around 1910. Motorman Frank Bear is leaning out the front window, and conductor Floyd Loomis is on the rear step. *Courtesy Washington County Museum.*

Forest Grove residents were being served by two modern electric interurban railroads, and there was no need to travel to Carnation to catch a train.

Crowds greeted the arrival of the first OE train to Forest Grove on November 15, 1908, as the beautiful Niles-built interurban cars rolled onto private right-of-way in front of the new OE depot on First Avenue and First Street (present-day Nineteenth Avenue and Ash Street). The OE kept a small two-bay carbarn across the street from the station.

There was also excitement when the modern steel Red Electrics inaugurated service to the tile-roofed SP depot on the corner of Main and Nineteenth Streets on January 17, 1914. The competing depots served slightly different needs. The OE service to Forest Grove was a nineteen-mile branch line from Garden Home, whereas the Red Electric route (twenty-six miles from Portland Union Station) was part of the West Side Line from Portland to Saint Joseph.

The arrival of the interurban lines caused a certain amount of friction with the Forest Grove Transportation Company, whose streetcars had to cross both mainlines, as evidenced by this court case:

> [The] *Forest Grove Transportation Company complained that the Oregon Electric Railway Company failed to observe the rules regarding crossings or the legal requirements concerning the same where said Oregon Electric Railway Company's line crosses plaintiff's track in Forest Grove. The matter was taken up with the Oregon Electric Railway Company and the general manager replied that, while he did not think conditions were as bad as represented, still there was no excuse for his cars not stopping at the crossing, and stated that trainmen failing thereafter to make the stop would be removed from the service. Complainant was so advised and the matter closed.*

Concerns over new electric interurbans—or, indeed, with automobiles—proved short-lived. In 1911, the Forest Grove Transportation Company ceased operation, and its tracks were removed from city streets. The event was belatedly reported in the *Electric Railway Review*: "Interests controlling the Forest Grove Transportation Company, a 2.7-mile [*sic*] line connecting Forest Grove and South Forest Grove with the Southern Pacific depot, have sold their stock, and the company has now gone out of business. No receiver was appointed."[89]

The Transportation Company had a contentious relationship with city leaders over the years, yet Forest Grove residents were proud of their street railway. Many rode it at first, as described in this August 1907 article in the *Washington County News-Times*: "The business has grown steadily until today the passenger car is carrying an average of 200 persons daily. The company has endeavored to do the very best for the traveling public and today Forest Grove is enjoying one of the best and most appreciable conveniences of any city in the state."[90]

When the lack of further need for a streetcar to Carnation convinced the Forest Grove Transportation Company to close up shop, it was a disappointment for many Forest Grove citizens. Their very own streetcar line was gone after five fleeting years.

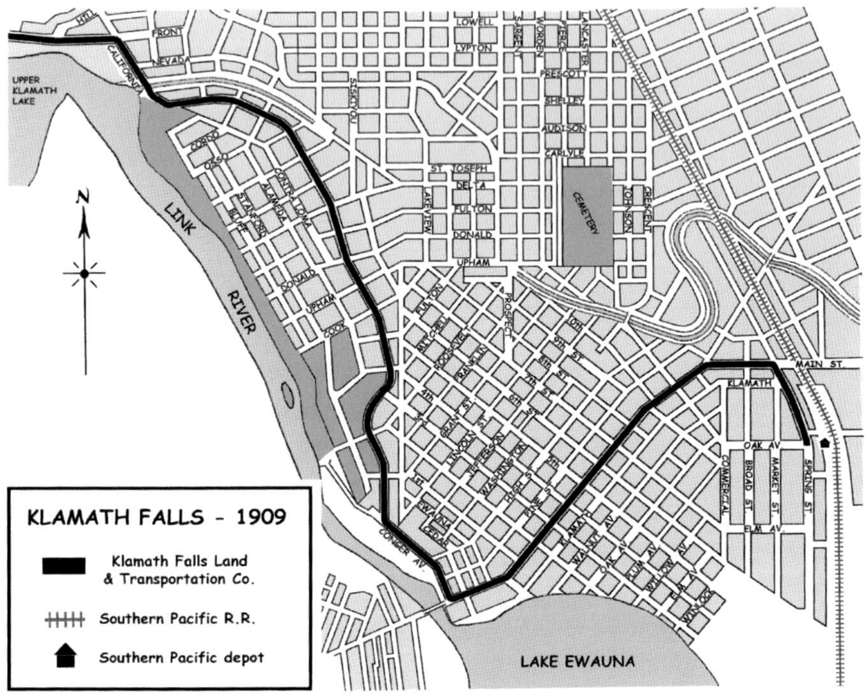

The Klamath Land and Transportation Company's three-and-a-half-mile railway ran from the railroad station, through the commercial district, to boat docks on Upper Klamath Lake. The carbarn that housed the railway's one streetcar and two horses was located near Conger Avenue and California Street. *Map by author.*

Chapter 8

KLAMATH FALLS, 1907–1911

In 1906, the Klamath Development Company, which was also involved in building a steam railroad into Klamath Falls, applied for authority to operate a streetcar from downtown to its Hot Springs Addition, near the future site of Klamath High School. The Klamath Canal Company sought a similar franchise for a streetcar line to its Buena Vista Addition, which was north of town along Upper Klamath Lake in the area bordered by California Avenue, Front Street and Buena Vista Street. With the Southern Pacific Railroad building toward Klamath Falls and two street railways planned, Jay Scott Taylor, editor of the *Klamath Falls Express*, predicted a rosy future for the city: "Klamath Falls is now making a rapid and substantial growth, said Mr. Taylor yesterday, we now have a population of 1,500, an electric light and power plant, a city water system and a telephone exchange. Two street railway companies have been granted franchise and one of the proposed car lines will be completed this year."[91]

Since the developers proposed to serve opposite ends of town, things might have worked out but for corporate greed and municipal bungling. The two streetcar routes came together in the commercial district along Main Street between Third Street and Conger Avenue, where dual track would have been required. Unfortunately, the city council insisted on single-track operation through this corridor, stipulating that the first company to lay tracks would be granted Main Street right-of-way, with the second company paying usage fees to the other. This "catch" in city approval of either railway turned their competition into municipal warfare.

The race for control of Main Street began with a $500 wager. Klamath Falls Development Company director Major Charles Worden bet William K. Brown, his counterpart at the Canal Company, that the Development Company would get its rails laid first:

> *The activity in realty and* [building], *by which Main Street has been rapidly transformed from scattering stores to an almost continuous line of business houses for more than a mile, have now led to truly metropolitan warfare between rival corporations holding franchises for street railways on the present principal business thoroughfare. The kernel of the nut seems to be that when the Klamath Development Company, an auxiliary of the* [California and] *Northeastern Railroad Company, was granted the first franchise it was not so restricted that any other company should be permitted use of the same tracks. But when, at a later date, the Klamath Canal Company was given a franchise, restrictions were imposed in such a way as to make the corporation subservient to the will of the people as represented by the Council.*[92]

Shipping railway equipment to Klamath Falls was not an easy task. Since the city still lacked a direct rail connection to the outside world, supplies would need to be shipped overland. The Development Company's D.B. Campbell repurposed six-horse teams from the Hot Springs project, sending them to Grass Lake, California, in search of railroad iron. When William Brown, of the Canal Company, found out about his rival's supposedly secret expedition, he managed to misdirect them to a slow route around Orr Lake while sending his own wagon teams to retrieve used rail from the much closer Pokegama Sugar Pine Lumber Company logging railroad. The Development Company's wagons became mired in mud, and its rails are said to remain somewhere in Northern California to this day.

As teams from both companies struggled toward Klamath Falls in June 1906, Brown hired every available workman to begin laying ties on Main Street. In order to avoid an injunction halting work, he paid them sixty cents per hour to work through a weekend. All was ready the next week, when wagons, pulled by exhausted horses, delivered railroad steel to the

Canal Company. Brown had won the bet, but the feud was not quite over. Klamath Development president A.H. Naftzger looked to the courts to regain the advantage:

> *At the end of one week, during which the Klamath Development Company has constructed track for a street railway over the greater portion of the disputed streets also desired by the Klamath Canal Company, which has built considerable track, a truce has been declared in the street conflict.*
>
> *It has been agreed that construction will be suspended pending the return of President A.H. Naftzger, of the Development Company, from New York, when terms of adjustment will be considered by the heads of the two corporations. The result seems to be a victory for the Development Company, an auxiliary of the* [California and] *Northeastern Railroad, and was arrived at in consequence of the arrival of G.N. Wendling of that corporation.*[93]

The Development Company threw in the towel not long after its competitors countered with their own work-stopping injunction in August 1906:

> *County Judge J.B. Griffith today granted a temporary injunction, on application of the Klamath Canal Company, restraining the Klamath Development Company from continuing the work of laying tracks for a street railway on Main Street, alleging that the franchise granted by the old City Council holding over after the adoption of the new charter for the city was invalid. The Klamath Canal Company secured a new charter from the present City Council and seeks the injunction upon the ground that the rival street railway company is not possessed of a legal franchise.*[94]

Canal Company subsidiary Klamath Land and Improvement Company began railway operation in 1907. Trial runs were made on April 13, when twenty guests and dignitaries rode from the corner of Main Street and Conger Avenue to Upper Klamath Lake. Public service was inaugurated on July 11, with commemorative tickets selling for $1.50. Streetcars operated on a fifteen-minute schedule for a fare of $0.05.

Having lost the race to lay the first rails, the Klamath Development Company abandoned plans to build a railway and turned its attention to

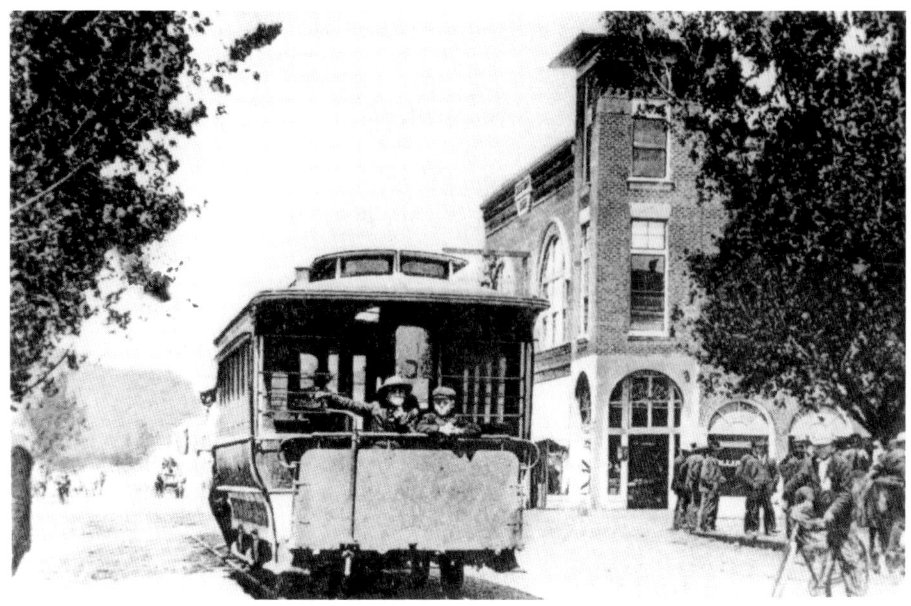

Circa 1910 view of the Klamath Land and Transportation Company horsecar headed east past the Hall Hotel on Main Street at Fourth Street. *Author's collection.*

the Hot Springs development. Roads through the area were paved and lots sold, and in 1911, the elegant, three-story White Pelican Hotel was opened. No rail had been laid into the Hot Spring Addition, and the partially constructed roadbed was never used.

The Klamath Land and Improvement Company railway grew to three and a half miles in length. In August 1907, tracks were laid across the new Government Canal Bridge to a northern terminus near the Upper Lake docks on Front Street. In 1909, an extension was made on the other end of the line, terminating beside the new Southern Pacific Railroad depot on Spring Street at Oak Avenue. The completed railway passed through the hotel and shopping districts as it carried passengers from the depot to the Upper Lake boat docks. The final route was somewhat different from that stipulated in the original franchise, running from Oak Avenue, north along Spring Street to Main Street, west on Main to Conger Avenue, north on Conger to California and then north on California to Front Street and along Front to approximately where the marina is today. The carbarn was located near Conger and California Avenues.

Charley Adams—the railway's one-man driver, conductor and maintenance engineer—remembered the horsecar line in a 1938 interview. He referred to it as the Linkville Trolley, which reflects the original name for the city of Klamath Falls:

> *"We had to make one trip a day to hold our franchise," said Charley. "sometimes that's all we did make. On quiet days I had lot of time to stop for a game of pool."*
>
> *Charley said that the biggest days came when pleasure crowds rode to the boat landing for trips on the Upper Lake. At those times the little old car would groan with an over-capacity load.*
>
> *Buck and Sealem, Charley said, were a lively pair of nags, which would run at the drop of a hat. They did their jobs well, however, and Charley became an expert at maneuvering the cumbersome trolley over the sidewalk crossings where the snow had been packed in against the rails. Sometimes, however, there was a derailment in true Toonerville Trolley style.*
>
> *Fare on the trolley was a nickel. Strangers could either take it or the regular hotel cabs from the depot. Charley sometimes showed the Negro cab drivers just how good he was at getting business, standing close to the step of the train and putting on a sales talk for the Linkville trolley as the passengers came out. The Lakeside Inn, the American House, and the Hotel Hall were leading hostelries in those days, and the trolley made stops at all of them.*
>
> *The regular fare was 5 cents, but sometimes, when Charley couldn't make change, he pocketed whatever his passengers gave him and let it go at that. Evan Reames was the president of the company that operated the trolley. At the end of each month Charley would turn over the receipts, take a check for his month's pay and that constituted the only business transaction necessary in operating the trolley.*[95]

Some viewed the horsecar, which had originally belonged to the Sutter Street Railway in San Francisco, as a temporary expedient. The city frequently asked when the streetcar would be converted to electric operation, but the railway company prevaricated, considering alternatives. President Evan R. Reames made a trip to San Francisco to investigate a gasoline-powered rail car but returned empty-handed. In the meantime, the only improvement seems to have been the installation of a new set of horsecar wheels (prompted by frequent derailments on the rough track).

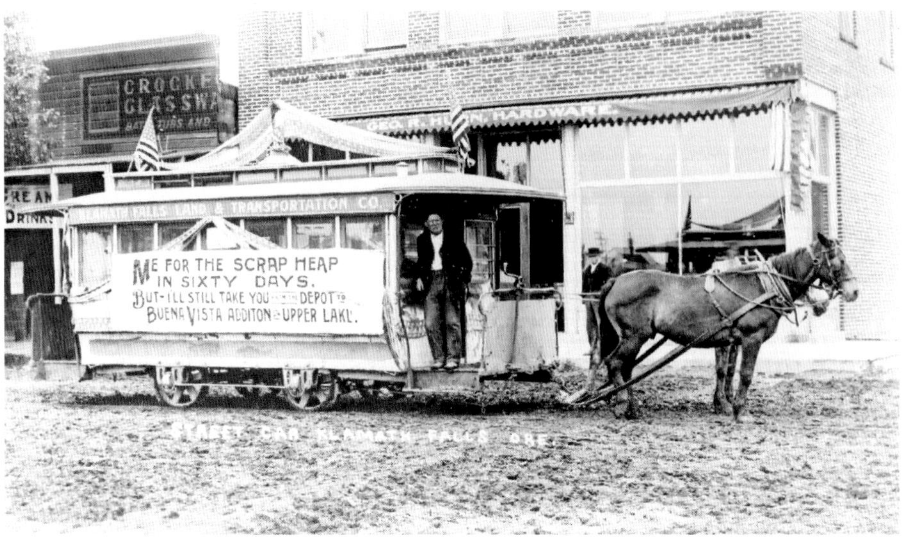

Driver Charley Adams leans out the platform of the Klamath Falls streetcar in front of the George Hurn Hardware Store on Main Street. It is July 4, 1910, and the little car is decorated for the holiday. The sign on the car reads, "Me for the scrap heap in sixty days. But—I'll still take you from the depot to Buena Vista Addition on Upper Lake." *Author's collection.*

In 1909, Reames finally applied for a franchise to electrify the railway, and the company's intention to upgrade its system was announced in the trade press:

> *E.R. Reames, president of the Klamath Falls Land & Transportation Company, announces that steps are being taken to electrify the street car system of that city. For the past two years the company has been operating horse cars. No contracts have been made for power but it is expected that the Moore power plant will supply all the necessary power.*[96]

One year later, the city presented the Transportation Company with an ultimatum: either modernize or lose the franchise. When the company failed to respond, the city revoked the charter. Ironically, Reames, who was also president of the Klamath Light and Power Company, had failed to arrange for an adequate source of electric power with which to improve the railway.

After regular operation ceased in the fall of 1910, the city briefly found itself in the streetcar business. Sources are not clear on how long municipal operation lasted, but it may have been several months, as crews did not begin removing rails from the streets until May 9, 1911.

Having lost continued financing from its predominantly Californian backers, the Klamath Falls streetcar system had come to an inglorious end. At three years, the Klamath Falls Land and Transportation operation became the shortest-lived of Oregon's small-town streetcar systems. Even so, the railway that seldom took in more than forty dollars per month would be fondly remembered for the important role it had played in spurring development.

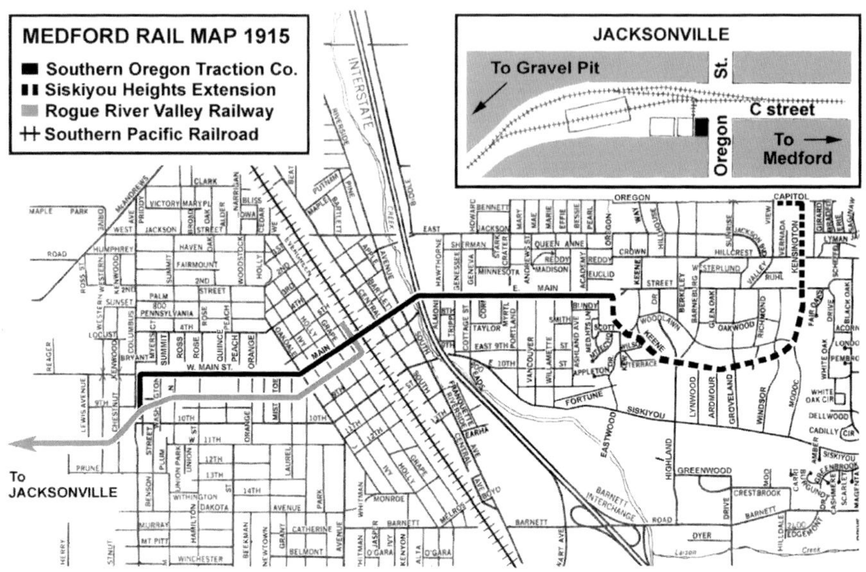

The Southern Oregon Traction Company opened the last small-town street railway in Oregon. This map shows its two-and-a-half-mile line running from Siskiyou Heights on the east to a junction with the Rogue River Valley Railroad on Ninth and Columbus in the west. In 1916, SOTCO absorbed the Rogue River Valley Railway and electrified six miles of track between Medford and Jacksonville. *Map modified from original by Bert Webber with permission.*

Chapter 9

MEDFORD-JACKSONVILLE, 1891/1914–1920

The history of electric railways in southwestern Oregon is really the tale of two companies: a traditional street railway and a steam short line that aspired to be an electric interurban railroad. The two intertwined their fates in a merger.

On July 15, 1913, a group of investors headed by Spencer S. Bullis organized the Southern Oregon Traction Company (SOTCO) to operate streetcars between the train depot in downtown Medford and a planned development on Siskiyou Heights. Its first trolley was tested on March 16, 1914, running east on East Main Street from the Southern Pacific Railroad (SP) depot and Eastwood Drive. Regular passenger service commenced on March 20. The fare was one nickel.

Two extensions were added during the first year, when some twenty thousand passengers rode the line. Construction was initially held up while arrangements were made for a crossing of the SP mainline. After the negotiations were successfully completed, the streetcar route was expanded westward, through the downtown business district, to Oakdale Avenue. Next, the Traction Company started laying track eastward toward Siskiyou Heights: "Work will be begun at once by this company on the extension of its lines from the Siskiyou Heights addition east and north to the city reservoir, about 1 mile. Further extension will be made if arrangements can be made with the property owners."[97]

The Siskiyou extension swung south around the hill on what is now Keene Way Drive and then back across Main Street, on present-day

Modoc Avenue and Kensington Square, to Capitol Avenue and then west along the edge of the city reservoir to a terminus near present-day Valley View Drive. In 1955, San Francisco rail historian David L. Stearns recalled a ride over the new tracks:

> *The day I was there in August 1914, the temperature was about 105°. Mr. Hall, proprietor of a garage back of the Medford Hotel took us for a ride around the valley to attempt to cool us off. That evening after dark, I recall* [some] *things about that line. It ran precisely at the S.P. crossing on Main Street (the car laid over there between runs). It ran east on Main to the foot of the hill then ran along the base of the bench below the Catholic hospital. The line had many curves beyond the hospital and that nice, new, single trucker* [streetcar] *jerked in rounding them.*
>
> *I recall we passed a brightly lighted building close to the track on our right and were told that was the clubhouse of the Medford Golf Course.*
>
> *Somewhere out in the Heights District, the line turned north then west and ended at the east side of a knoll crowned by a reservoir. The motorman urged us to walk up to and around the reservoir for a view out over the valley. We did so and when he had changed ends* [to operate from the other end of the streetcar] *he joined us and spent some time pointing out the sights to us.*
>
> *On the return trip, the car stopped near the Golf Club sort of automatically (I suppose it was about 8 or 9 o'clock); the lights inside the building were turned out one-by-one and then the building was all dark. We just sat there. Soon a man emerged and boarded the car.*
>
> *We had been the only passengers on the car during the outbound trip and had become quite chummy with the motorman, and he now introduced the new passenger as the pro at the Golf Club.*
>
> *In view of the leisurely nature of the trip we took that evening, I assume the line had about an hourly schedule at that time of day.*[98]

Bullis quickly regretted having let real estate promoters talk him into extending the streetcar line into Siskiyou Heights. He determined that development there would proceed too slowly to produce expected fare box revenue and bailed out. Operation to the Siskiyou Heights terminal was discontinued in 1915.

Bullis then turned his attention to the opposite end of town, as he was in the process of purchasing the railroad linking Medford with Jacksonville:

> *Bullis in the meantime had obtained control of the Rogue River Valley Railway and announced plans to electrify that road to Jacksonville and beyond into the mining and timber region to the west. To facilitate the work, Bullis ordered the Siskiyou Heights extension, about a mile, removed and relaid on the west side on Main Street, to connect with the steam road on the outskirts of town, and by October, 1915 all necessary rail was at hand and the overhead was being strung on the new track.*[99]

Rail from the discontinued Siskiyou Heights route was used to extend the railway westward on Main Street, from the SP depot. Overall track length remained two miles, running from a terminus west of Bear Creek at North Riverside Avenue, along East and West Main Street, to Elm Street. Before long, four more blocks of track would be added down Elm Street to Eighth Street, where a connection was made with the Rogue River Valley Railway line to Jacksonville. Removing the rails from the Siskiyou Heights extension was not a daunting task, since the ties were sitting on un-ballasted dirt. In fact, the first streetcar "mishap," a 1915 empty car derailment, was attributed to the unimproved roadbed on that line:

> *The Bullis street car jumped the track near Jayne's crossing this morning at seven o'clock. The car escaped the control of the motorman on a curve and was derailed, the trolley wheel dropping off. The accident was caused by weeds overgrowing the rails. They made the track slippery. The motorman put sand on the track when he realized his difficulty, and applied the current for ahead. Instead the car went backwards and the derailment followed. There were no passengers at the time of the accident. In over a year of operation this is the first mishap.*[100]

SOTCO is thought to have had three streetcars, all of which were operated by one-man crews. No. 1 was a classic single-truck Birney Safety Car built by the St. Louis Car Company in 1914. No. 2 was another single-truck Birney built in 1915. It was purchased to handle the increased schedule necessitated by the RRVR merger.[101] The two Birneys were double-ended PAYE (pay-as-you-enter) cars accommodating thirty-four passengers. The third streetcar, originally numbered 220, was a single-end, double-truck car built by Kuhlman in 1902. It seated fifty-six, with room for another forty standees. Prior to its 1915 acquisition by SOTCO, this former Cleveland trolley had been remodeled, with the addition of longer prepayment platforms and a deck roof. Further modifications, including the addition of a second trolley

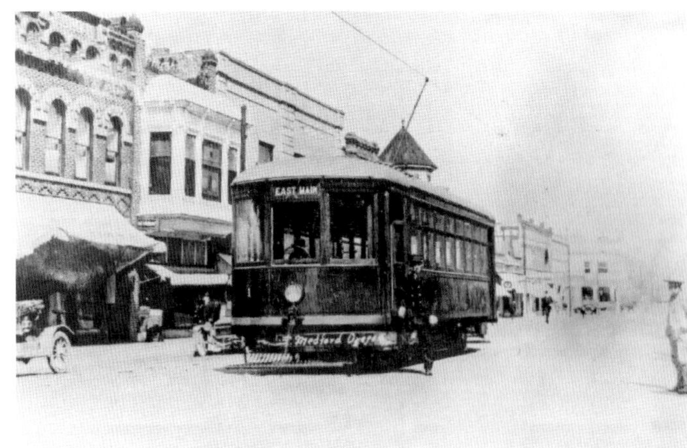

Southern Oregon Traction Company Birney car No. 1 is seen on Main Street circa 1915. The car is headed west but is incorrectly signed for the eastern terminus of Medford's street railway. *Author's collection.*

pole and another controller, were made upon arrival in Medford to allow double-end operation.

Photographic evidence for these cars is elusive; only Birney No. 1 is seen operating on Medford city streets. There are no snapshots of Birney No. 2, and the only pictures of No. 220, taken after the abandonment of passenger service, show a deteriorated body with motors, controllers and wheels removed: "The double-truck car was completely out of operation. It was stored on a spur along the main (line) just west of the junction where the trolley cut into the steam tracks in the west edge of Medford."[102]

Building a street railway had been the first step in a grand scheme. Spencer Bullis, and his son, Seth, wanted to build an electric interurban empire, with Medford as its hub. Branch lines would have run south to Ashland, north to Eagle Point and west to Grants Pass, as reported in the June 1914 *Electric Railway Journal*:

> *This company has completed 1 mile of track in Medford and plans to build 3 miles of new track within the next six months. It will purchase power from the California-Oregon Power Company, Medford. This railway will ultimately connect Medford, Siskiyou Heights, Phoenix, Talent, Ashland and Central Point. S.M. Bullis, Medford, President.*[103]

Bullis was acting on those plans when he obtained control of the financially troubled Rogue River Valley Railway (RRVR). The merger expanded SOTCO to 8.19 miles of track—2.50 of which were in Medford and its suburbs.[104] The Traction Company's long-range plans were even more extensive:

> [The] *Southern Oregon Traction Company* [incorporated] *July 15, 1913 in Ore., and on July 1, 1915, purchased the Rogue River Valley Ry....* [The] *Line of road extends from* [the John] *Opp Mine to* [the] *City Reservoir, passing through Jacksonville and Medford, Ore., 9.5 miles. The line is projected to the California State Line, a total distance of about 35 miles. Gauge, 4 ft. 9 in. Rails, 56 and 75 lbs. The road is operated by overhead trolley, except about 3 miles of track which are operated by steam for freight only. Locomotives, 2; motor cars* [closed], *2; combination cars, 2; freight cars, 14.*[105]

The RRVR was a much older enterprise than SOTCO, having started on January 16, 1891, as a steam short line. For most of its life, both before and after Spencer Bullis, the RRVR was managed by businessman William S. Barnum. Like other railroad entrepreneurs of the time, he would also be remembered for erecting a hotel to serve travelers. The fifty-seven-room Grand Hotel at the northeast corner of North Front and Fifth Streets in Medford opened in 1915.

The RRVR was successor to the Medford and Jacksonville Railroad Company, which had been founded in 1890 by a group of businessmen desirous of establishing a connection with the mainline railroad that had bypassed Jacksonville. Since the new town of Medford was served by the Oregon and California Railroad, a contract was made with Honeyman, DeHart and Company (later the Honeyman Hardware Company) of Portland for building and operating a short line linking the two cities.

While the RRVR awaited delivery of its first locomotive, and a handsome baggage express car, trial runs were made with equipment rented from the Union Pacific Railroad. When everything seemed satisfactory, those in charge looked forward to a successful business. Indeed, the diminutive railroad carried on a promising trade at first, departing J-ville with bricks from the kiln west of town, beer from its five breweries and ladies heading for a day of shopping and returning with goods transferred from the SP depot in Medford, as well as lawyers bound for the Jacksonville Courthouse (Jacksonville was the county seat until 1927).

But the RRVR's first locomotive proved a disappointment. The steady five-mile climb from Medford back to Jacksonville proved too much for the little ten-ton engine. No. 1, a 2-4-2T locomotive built by the H.K. Porter Company in December 1890, was designed for nearly flat rights-of-way, like the Manhattan Elevated Railway in New York. So, in 1895, it was sold to the street railway company in Albany, Oregon. The half dozen other locomotives used on the RRVR over the years proved better suited for its short-haul freight trains, although they were a bit expensive and slow when it came to passenger service.

Barnum began improvements to the Jacksonville-Medford line, financed by a $100,000 stock offering. A handsome depot was erected at C and Oregon Streets in 1891 (it was replaced with a newer station in 1908), and additions were made to rolling stock. In 1905, he pioneered "modern" passenger service by adding a seven-passenger Fairbanks "auto car" to the roster. The new-fangled car made three daily round trips between Jacksonville and Medford. Fare for the six-mile, fifteen-minute journey was twenty-five cents. The auto car was a "quick service" supplement to the steam train, which continued to operate, taking twenty-five minutes to make the trip.

In 1909, a larger gasoline-powered rail car, designed by son William Henry Barnum, was added to the roster. This product of the Ferry Garage Company of San Francisco had a wooden body over a steel frame, accommodating twenty-two passengers in the main cabin and six in the smoking section. Its seventy-horsepower, four-cylinder Brennan engine produced a top speed of thirty-five miles per hour. The San Francisco rail car cost $5,000 but was said to have operated at one-tenth the cost of a steam locomotive.

The next challenge for the RRVR was competition from taxis. The company's desire to prevent these so-called jitney cars from stealing its customers was understandable, given the business climate of the time. Aggressive jitney drivers posed a problem for street railway companies in several U.S. cities, including Portland, where uninsured, non-union drivers drove ahead of streetcars, trawling for passengers, who would then be charged a lower fare. The Portland

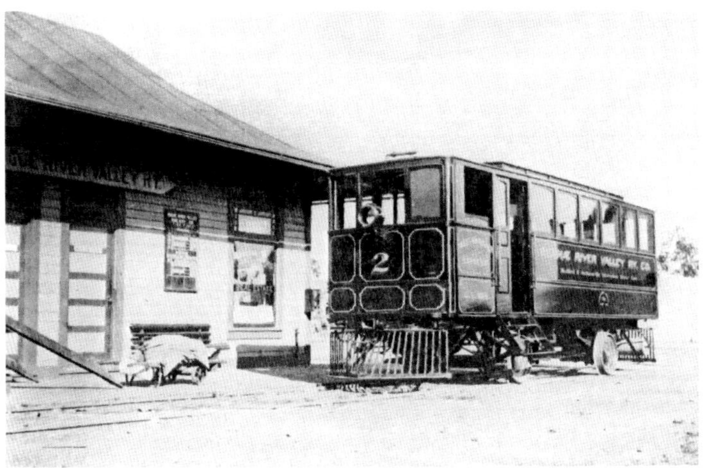

Rogue River Valley No. 2, a rail gasoline car designed by William S. Barnum's son, William, in 1909, featured separate passenger, baggage and smoking compartments. It is seen here in front of the Medford depot. *Bert Webber Collection.*

Railway, Light and Power Company eventually won an injunction against this form of unregulated competition. In Jacksonville, jitneys, known as auto stages, faded from the scene after the city imposed a license fee:

> *Jacksonville is up in arms over a recent ruling of the City Council that auto stages running from that city to Medford should pay $20 a month tax.*
>
> *First, Mayor T.T. Shaw resigned, and now the women have held an indignation meeting and charge that the Council has been influenced by the Barnum Railroad, which is the only transportation line between the two places, in an effort to kill off competition.*
>
> *The owners of the railroad declare they had nothing to do with the Council's action, but that it was a move calculated to protect a Jacksonville corporation against the encroachments of Medford autoists.*[106]

As the hauling of goods and fresh fruit increased, connecting tracks were built in Medford to allow the interchange of freight between the SOTCO and SP. A lack of industrial sites (and, eventually, a decline) kept this trade small, but the interchanging of boxcars was far less labor intensive than loading and reloading cargo at the Medford depot.

Trolley service on the Medford-Jacksonville line commenced on January 1, 1916, with energy purchased from the California-Oregon Power Company. Six hundred volts of DC current was produced by a 250-kilowatt Westinghouse motor generator in the Highland Park substation. The electric streetcars were less expensive to operate than steam trains and allowed for a more flexible service over the six miles of single track. During the steam railroad days, only one stop, at Perrydale Station, was allowed on the RRVR. Now, more frequent stops were possible, since there was not so much concern over fuel consumption and braking.

Approximately three miles of track remained under steam-only operation. A locomotive was retained for occasional freight train use, such as hauling rock from the quarry two miles west of Jacksonville and serving a lumber mill for which a spur had been built at West Eleventh and Jeanette Streets in Medford. Meanwhile, the gas-powered rail cars were sold to the Pacific and Eastern Railroad, which put them to use on its thirty-three-mile run between Medford and the little mill town of Butte Falls.

No. 1, "the little engine that couldn't," was the only RRVR steam locomotive to escape the scrap heap. The dinky engine changed hands a number of times before returning to Jacksonville. In 1895, it is said to have been sold to the Albany Street Railway, which removed the saddle tank and rebuilt it as an

0-4-2T locomotive (see chapter on Albany). In 1905, it went to Skelly Lumber Company, where it was transformed into an 0-4-0T engine before being badly burned in a 1911 fire and abandoned.[107] The wreck was later salvaged for use by two lumber companies before being rebuilt by California train enthusiasts. Then, in 2014, the owners of a Jacksonville event center facilitated the return of RRVR No. 1 after an absence of 119 years. The historic engine now on display next to the 1908 schoolhouse on Bigham's Knoll is the only surviving small-town street railway vehicle in Oregon.

After electrification, the favored vehicle for the Jacksonville-Medford run was the double-truck Cleveland streetcar, which offered a larger passenger capacity and a smoother ride than the Birneys. However, even with this larger streetcar, the line between Medford and Jacksonville was not an interurban railway:

> *Southern Oregon Traction Company did not become an "interurban," according to the classic definition of an interurban line, just because it bought the Rogue River Valley Railway which ran between two towns. For all practical purposes, SOTCO remained a city street traction company merely with an extended line into the country. Although there were true "interurban" railways in other parts of the nation with short milage* [sic] *runs, those short hauls were often parts of greater inter-city systems.*[108]

As it turned out, the additional electrification would prove costly to SOTCO, bringing an end to hopes for an interurban network. Business in once-thriving Jacksonville was on the decline, and more affordable automobiles, driving over improved roads, resulted in dwindling ridership. With the suburban streetcar operating at a loss, Bullis was unable to repay the high-interest loans with which the Jacksonville line electrification had been financed. Like August Lovegren in Cherry Grove, Bullis had invested in new technology. This time, however, the price was too high.

In 1918, SOTCO was forced into bankruptcy, and William S. Barnum (who had retained the mortgage) returned as executive, albeit with improved rolling stock and an electrified railroad. While searching for new buyers, he continued passenger service. During the ensuing half-dozen years, the railroad was sold from one new owner to another, all the while losing money. As each hapless manager fell behind in mortgage payments, SOTCO ownership reverted to Barnum.

J.T. Gagnon bought the railway in 1920 and reorganized it as the Medford Coast Railroad. As he struggled with worn-out equipment and roadway, regularly scheduled passenger service was dropped. The rolling stock had deteriorated badly by this time. All of the streetcars suffered from burned-out motors that restricted their operating speeds, and a dent in the front end of Birney No. 1 carried a temporary patch held in place by unpainted two-by-fours.

In 1922, John Opp, owner of a quartz mine west of Jacksonville, took over operation with a promise to restore streetcar operation. That effort was brought to a halt after a fire burned the Highland Park substation to the ground.

Complaints from city councils in the two towns had not fallen on deaf ears, as when Gagnon took over again in February 1924, he also intended to start streetcar operation again. Nevertheless, that did not happen. The substation producing the railway's power was never rebuilt, making the discontinuance of streetcar service permanent. A freight-only service soldiered on with steam locomotives until April 1, 1925.

By 1925, another failure to meet mortgage payments had again returned control of the Medford Coast Railroad to Barnum, who had no desire to restore operation. On July 28, he asked the Oregon Public Utilities Commission for the right to abandon the railroad and dismantle it. In response, the state stipulated that he sell for scrap value to anyone willing to continue using the railroad.

A compromise was reached in which the City of Medford agreed to buy the railroad for $11,000. Officials seem to have been persuaded by the possibility of hauling gravel for city projects from the quarry west of Jacksonville (which Barnum owned). So, for a few months, Medford's railway, like its neighbor to the east, Klamath Falls, was under municipal ownership. However, no gravel had been moved by April of the following year, when the city rethought the situation and began liquidating its railroad. In a twist of fate, some of the rail salvaged from city streets was used for sign posts directing automobile traffic. More vestiges of the old RRVR disappeared in 1929, when the roundhouse and yards in Jacksonville were razed. W.S. Barnum had passed away the previous year.

In their classic book on interurban railway history, professors George Hilton and John Due refer to the Southern Oregon Traction Company as one of the "worst examples" of interurban building.[109] Indeed, it had been built after the boom in electric railway construction was waning, and it remained too short to generate a profit. That being said, the Southern Oregon Traction Company had earned its place in history as the last of Oregon's street railways to begin operation. The street railway in Medford was electric from the start, and it tripled in length by incorporating a suburban service to a neighboring town. It also survived for nine years, which was longer than several of Oregon's small-town railways.

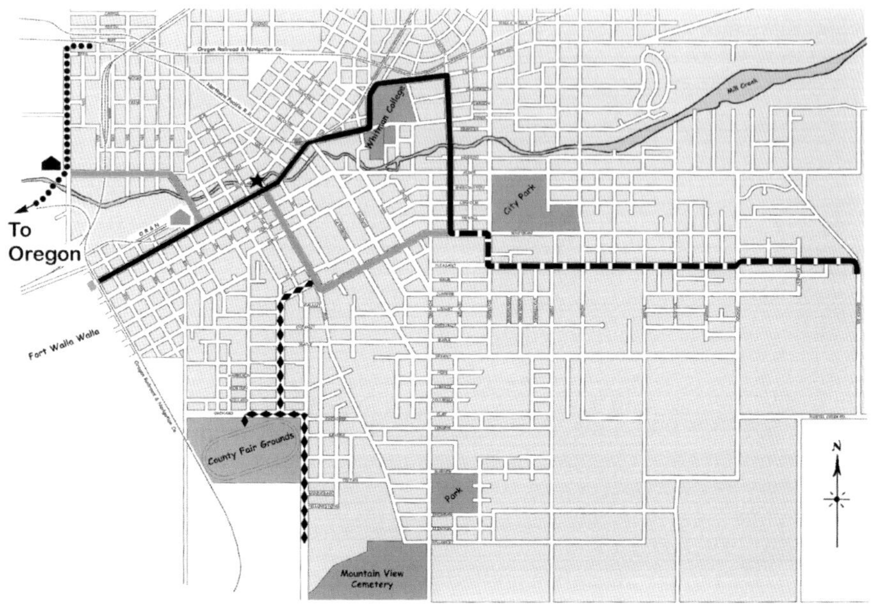

WALLA WALLA VALLEY TRACTION CO.

- City Park Line (1906)
- East Walla Walla Line (1908)
- Prospect Heights Line (1908)
- Track shared by multiple lines
- City Lines Terminal
- Milton & Freewater Interurban (1907)
- Interurban depot
- Carbarn

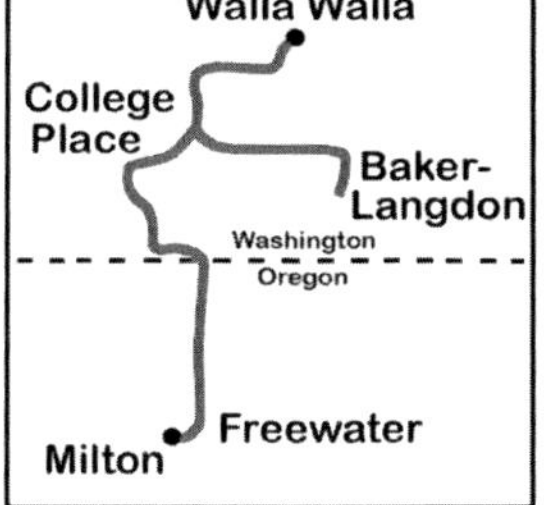

At its peak around 1908, the Walla Walla Valley Traction Company operated 8.09 miles of city street railway lines, as well as a 14.00-mile interurban line to Freewater and Milton. At 5.51 miles, tracks in the state of Oregon accounted for nearly 40 percent of the interurban system. *Map by author.*

Chapter 10

MILTON-FREEWATER, 1907–1931

Milton and Freewater, independent cities until merging in 1950, were once part of an interurban railway based across the border in Walla Walla, Washington. While the five miles of track in Oregon was not a city streetcar line, an exception is made for including its story here since it provided an important trolley connection for two small Oregon towns.

The Walla Walla Street Railway and Investment Company was incorporated on February 18, 1889, to provide street railway service in the southeastern Washington city of Walla Walla. The first horse-drawn streetcars began running there, from Second and Main Streets to the end of Park Street, in 1890.

By the end of the first year, banker and merchant William Parkhurst Winans had expanded the railway to four miles of track, six streetcars and twenty-four horses. Nonetheless, in spite of a $100,000 stock offering, the enterprise did not thrive. Plans to convert the system to electric operation were thwarted around 1899, when the modest operation ceased operation. It would be some time before streetcar wheels would turn again in Walla Walla.

The next player in the Garden City transit saga was one Edwin S. Isaacs, who organized the Walla Walla City Railway Company in 1901 for the express purpose of building an electric railway. The start of construction on six miles of track was announced with much fanfare in March 1902:

> *E.S. Isaacs, of Walla Walla, has been granted a twenty-five-year franchise by the county commissioners for ten feet of the roadway on county roads near the city*

for the operation of an interurban motor line in connection with the street railway line which he purposes to operate in this city. It is likely that as soon as electric power can be obtained from the plant on the Walla Walla river. Mr. Isaacs and his associates will begin construction of a street car line in Walla Walla.[110]

Such predictions proved overly optimistic. The City Railway never did launch trolley service. Things had been held up by the search for a source of power sufficient for an electric railway. That energy did not become available until a hydroelectric plant was completed on the Walla Walla River on December 31, 1904. However, the delay did not fret the powerful utility interests behind railroad building in Walla Walla. On May 17, 1905, they reorganized the City Railway as the Walla Walla Valley Traction Company (WWVT), with gas and electric utilities executive Isaac W. Anderson named president and Edwin Isaacs vice-president:

Another step toward fulfilling the promise made by Isaac W. Anderson to build a street car system in Walla Walla was taken at the meeting of the Walla Walla Traction company held at the offices of the Northwestern Gas & Electric company Wednesday night, when organization was perfected, officers and directors elected and Isaac W. Anderson, the newly elected president, was authorized to close contracts for ties, rails and street car material and also to employ engineers to survey out the line within the business and residence districts.[111]

The reinvigorated company expected to complete an electric city railway within six months, and this time, the prognostication proved accurate. Trolleys began running between the Oregon Railway and Navigation depot and City Park on December 24, 1906.

The addition of two more city lines in 1908 was greeted as a great improvement: "Walla Walla now has a street railway system that is in every way a credit. This is well, too, for there is nothing that gives a city more prestige and which adds so much to the comfort and convenience of its citizens than up-to-date street railway transportation."[112]

From 1908 until the first abandonments in 1920, the Walla Walla system had three city streetcar lines, all of which either terminated, or passed, South Second Avenue and East Main Street, in the heart of the business district. Transfers available on all lines meant that passengers could ride to any part of the city for a single five-cent fare.

The City Park Line, later known as the "Loop" Line, served two train depots and City Park. It ran from the Oregon Railroad and Navigation Company depot (near Twelfth Avenue) up West Main Street to Second Avenue, south on South Second Avenue, east on Whitman Street, north on South Clinton Street (two blocks from City Park), west on East Isaacs Avenue, south on College Avenue (now Park Street), west on Boyer Avenue to the Northern Pacific Railroad depot and then west on East Main, crossing to West Main again.

The East Walla Walla Line shared the loop tracks to Whitman and Clinton Streets and then ran out Whitman to Division, down Division to Pleasant and out Pleasant Street to a terminus near the Ulysses H. Berney Mansion on Berney Drive. Mr. Berney was a prominent wholesale fruit grower, landowner and chairman of the school district. Rapid development of real estate in east Walla Walla was made possible by the new carline.

Like the East Walla Walla Line, the Prospect Heights Line ran from a terminal at East Main Street and South Second Avenue to the development for which it was named. Along the way, it gave access to the County Fairgrounds and a cemetery. The Prospect Heights Line shared tracks south on South Second to Eagan Street and then west on Eagan to South Fourth Avenue, south on Fourth to the Fairgrounds (a spur ran into the Fairgrounds), east on Orchard Street to South Third Avenue and then south on South Third Street to present-day Bandra Drive in Prospect Heights. The line terminated four blocks from Mountain View Cemetery:

> *This makes a delightful half hour's ride. Persons wishing to go to the cemetery take this line which lands them about four blocks from the necropolis. It can be easily seen that this line will prove a popular one. The addition it reaches has been divided up into city lots and it won't be long before it will have a substantial patronage.*[113]

No sooner had Walla Walla streetcars begun running than plans were afoot for the addition of an interurban division. The city franchise had been secured as part of a broader scheme to build an electric line to the twin border cities of Milton and Freewater in Oregon.

As the Traction Company turned its attention southward through the Walla Walla Valley, the prospect of interurban service was met with great enthusiasm in Milton:

> *The Walla Walla Valley Traction Company now has its track laid down to the head of Main street in this city, and it will be only a few days when there will be hourly service between this city and Walla Walla, Wash. This will be a great benefit to Milton and vicinity and will materially aid the already rapid growth of Milton. This city is now in a very prosperous condition; all*

> *the principal streets are being brought to proper grade, and many changes for the better have recently taken place. There will soon be a $16,000 hotel erected.*[114]

Work crews reached the southern terminus of the line at Milton on March 17, 1907. One month later, as construction was finishing up, a special train took dignitaries to Freewater, just across the city line from the neighboring town:

> *Interurban transportation between the city and Freewater is at last a reality. The first car made the round trip today with many of the prominent officials of the Walla Walla Valley Traction Company on board. The car left the local station at 7:03 o'clock, returning at 8:45. Hereafter the car will make the trip every two hours during the day, leaving Walla Walla at 7 A.M. and each odd hour thereafter. Returning, the car will leave Freewater on the even hours up to 8 P.M.*[115]

According to local lore, Freewater was formed as an independent town because the sale of alcohol was prohibited in its older neighbor. At any rate, since their town centers were only a few blocks apart, the Walla Walla Traction Company only built one depot, in Freewater. Accounts of the arrival of the interurban railway there were understandably positive, since the arrival of the interurban brought lifestyle changes to residents of eastern Oregon and Washington:

> *It has started a new era for Walla Walla; that of rapid and sure locomotion. People between the two towns now have a way of going shopping. No more hitching up the horses and a cold ride in the winter or a dusty one in the summer. They can board a car which passes their station every hour and, after a ride of 45 minutes, if they live in Milton and a corresponding shorter time at each successive station, they can do their shopping in Walla Walla and return any time of the day. The system facilitates much business in all directions.*
>
> *All along the line are signs of building and general prosperity. Houses are going up and suburban life will be a delight. Property has advanced and is still advancing as people realize the advantages that are right at their front doors.*[116]

The WWVT was doing well when it was leased to the Northwest Gas and Electric Company on July 1, 1907. By 1909, nearly 1 million passengers were being carried between Walla Walla and Milton each year. Soon, the railway came to the attention of giant East Coast combines jostling for control of utilities and railways throughout Oregon and Washington.

On September 1, 1909, Northwest Gas and Electric Company became part of Pennsylvania-based Northwestern Corporation, whose vast holdings included the electric light and street railway system in Walla Walla; the interurban line to Milton and Freewater; and electric, gas or water utilities in Albany, Corvallis, Eugene, Dallas, Independence, Lewiston, North Yakima, Pendleton and Springfield.[117] General Manager Alvadore Welch explained that Northwestern intended to build an electric railway between Salem and Eugene and possibly between Salem and Portland. In fact, Welch's Willamette Valley Company was already organizing railway franchises throughout the Willamette Valley (see chapters on Albany, Salem and Eugene):

> *Three lines* [are] *projected. The company has begun the development of a water power plant on the Mackenzie River which will generate 10,000 horsepower and the electric railway of Eugene, also controlled by the company, is projected to Albany and Salem. Prior to the sale, the building of the Eugene-Albany line was practically assured and the corporation was endeavoring to interest capital in an extension through to Portland.*
>
> *Another of the announced plans of the Northwest Corporation, which it is supposed will be carried out by the new purchasers, is the extension of the Walla Walla Valley traction line to La Grande.*[118]

In the summer of 1908, the WWVT drew up its own proposal for an extension of its lines in Oregon: "All doubt concerning the Walla Walla Valley Electric Company's intention to extend its interurban line from Milton to Athena was set at rest today when 16 right-of-way deeds were placed on file in the office of the county recorder. The deeds are all across land lying between Milton and Athena and extend to the very heart of the wheat belt."[119]

This was during the heyday for interurban building, so it is not surprising to find new companies were also entering the fray. In 1908, the Walla Walla and Columbia Traction Company was arranging rights-of-way for a proposed sixty-mile electric line connecting the cities of Dayton, Huntsville, Waitsburg, Prescott, Walla Walla, Milton, Freewater, Touchet and Wallua,[120] and in 1909, the Washington Traction Company had incorporated "to construct a system of electric railways radiating out of Walla Walla to various parts of Washington, Oregon and Idaho."[121]

In spite of all of these machinations, the proposed branches to Athena and La Grande were never built, nor were competing long-distance electric railroads. The WWVT remained the sole electric railway operator, with fourteen miles of interurban track.

The year 1910 brought two more changes of ownership and a final change in name. On May 11, the holdings of the Northwestern Corporation east of the Cascade Mountains were divided between the Columbia Light and Power Company and the Walla Walla Valley Railway Company, the gas and electric property going to the former and the traction holdings to the latter. This was followed on September 29 by the sale of Columbia Light and Power and the Walla Walla Valley Railway to Portland-based Pacific Power and Light Company (PP&L). The Oregon utility obtained a new franchise for the WWVT and renamed it the Walla Walla Valley Railway (WWV). PP&L had experience in the electric railway field, since it also ran the street railway system in Astoria, Oregon.

Throughout the 1910s, operation on the 8.09-mile city system in Walla Walla remained pretty much the same. Half-hour headways throughout the day were tightened up during rush hours with the addition of extra cars. During the morning rush, fifteen-minute service was maintained, using two streetcars. A third car was added for the afternoon rush, allowing ten-minute headways.

On the interurban division, hourly passenger service was provided between Walla Walla and Milton, from 6:00 a.m. until midnight daily. The last car left Walla Walla at 11:00 p.m. The big yellow interurbans, geared for forty miles per hour, made the trip in forty-five minutes, with a short layover at each end of the line. Stations included Walla Walla, College Place, Baker-Langdon, State Line, Ferndale, Freewater and Milton. The last three stops were in Oregon.

In addition to passenger service, the WWVT developed a profitable short-line freight business. Gradually, freight service became the most important source of revenue, and new electric locomotives known as "box motors" were purchased to haul carloads of fruit, dairy products and wheat in competition with the mainline railroads.

The interurban passenger and freight depot was located on the corner of West Main Street and South Seventh Avenue in Walla Walla. The carbarn and repair shops for both the city and interurban divisions were at what is now West Cherry Street and North Thirteenth Avenue. An attractive brick depot, office and two-story powerhouse were at the other end of the line, in Freewater, Oregon. The old station is still standing today at 403 Robbins Street in Milton-Freewater.

Service on the interurban line was described in a 1908 trade magazine:

> *On the interurban line we run an hourly schedule between Walla Walla, Milton and Freewater. There is a park at the Walla Walla River Station, which is about six miles out and which is the only place of amusement on the line. We*

run a half-hour schedule in the evenings and Sunday afternoons. The interurban line is 15 miles in length. On this line we use two 31'8" Brill patented semi-convertible combination passenger and baggage motor cars mounted on Brill patented No. 27-G1 trucks, two 12-seat open trail cars mounted on similar trucks, and the two new big 36' closed vestibule combination passenger and smoking motor cars mounted on Brill parented No. 27-E1 trucks.

Two regular freight trains are run daily. The first leaves Walla Walla at 7.45 A.M and the second at 1.40 P.M. There are frequent sidings along the line, which vary in capacity from two to ten cars, and the company has track connection and a traffic arrangement with the Northern Pacific. Recently during the berry season the Northern Pacific Railroad ran an express car over the line of the traction company.[122]

The WWVT roster had grown to eight cars by 1908. City service was provided by one twenty-eight-foot single-truck Brill semi-convertible, three thirty-six-foot double-truck semi-convertibles and two twelve-bench double-truck open trailers. The interurban fleet included two forty-one-foot Brill combination passenger and baggage motors and one two-hundred-horsepower box motor. The city cars accommodated twenty-eight, thirty-six and seventy-two passengers respectively, and the interurban "combos" held forty-six. All rolling stock was built by either the J.G. Brill Company in Philadelphia or the American Car Company (a Brill subsidiary) in St. Louis. Electrical equipment was General Electric. Walla Walla's first trolley was manufactured in 1906, and its last, the two interurbans, arrived in 1908.

In 1916, five of Walla Walla's city streetcars were remodeled so that they could be operated by one man (as in other cities, crews had previously included a conductor and motorman). Around the time staffing was reduced, the inventory of trolleys was the highest. By 1918, ten semi-convertible cars provided city service, while two passenger cars, two combines, three box motors, one steeplecab and eight freight cars served the interurban line. Two open trailers were used for suburban service to parks. In the early years, they also saw use on the run to Oregon. Six years later, the burden of service was carried by five city cars and two interurbans. Other vehicles, although remaining on the roster, were stored inactive in the Walla Walla yard.

Two city streetcar lines, to Prospect Heights and east Walla Walla, were discontinued on August 1, 1920, when the franchise agreement with the city expired. The street railway had not paid expenses for several years, and PP&L sought to focus on its electric power business. The last city trolley line in Walla Walla, City Park, ceased operation on December 31, 1926.

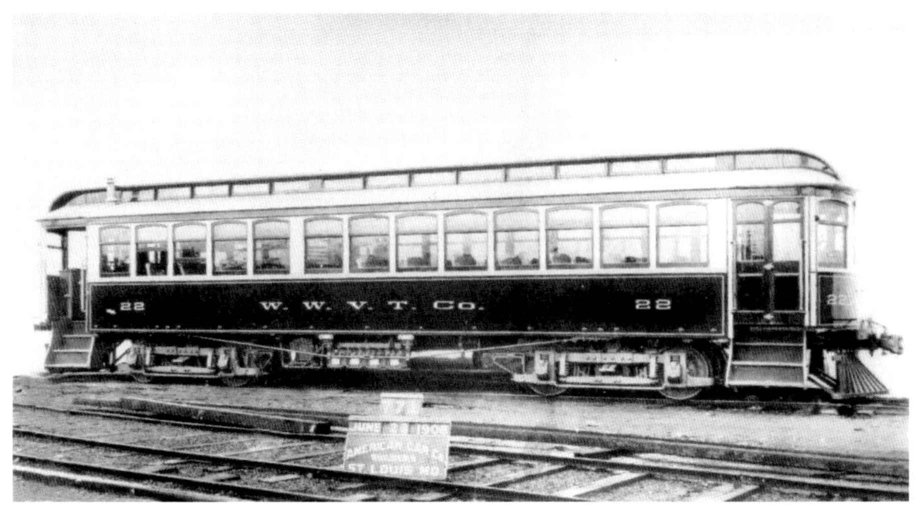

This builder's photograph of Walla Walla Valley Traction Company interurban No. 22 was taken at the American Car Company factory in St. Louis, Missouri, on June 23 1908. *George Chope Collection.*

The Northern Pacific Railroad (NP) purchased the WWV from PP&L in 1922. While the city streetcar lines were being discontinued, the interurban railway had persevered because of its profitable freight business:

> *The Walla Walla Valley Railway company, which gives street car service to Walla Walla and has an interurban line to Milton and Freewater, Or., was purchased yesterday by the Northwestern Improvement company, a subsidiary of the Northern Pacific Railway company, from the Pacific Power & Light company interests of this city…*
>
> *The power and light company desired no longer to handle the transportation lines at Walla Walla, but the deal in no way complicated its power and light holdings. For many years the traffic arrangements have been closed with the Northern Pacific. The purchase price was not given out. The electric railway company operates over 27 miles of city and interurban trackage.*[123]

The NP added two new interurban branches; however, they were freight-only, surely a sign that passenger service was becoming less important. The 4.4-mile Yellow Hawk branch from College Place to the Baker-Langdon orchards opened in 1923, and a line between Milton and Umapine, Oregon, followed in 1924. The rapidly growing freight service was now being impeded by interurban passenger trains:

> *Following purchase by NP, electric passenger traffic on the WWV became increasingly hampered by freight operations. While able to handle a few interurban cars lightly skipping along the 60-lb. rail, the power supply system was ill equipped to keep up with the heavier freight trains which now traveled the line. Old-timers recall instances where passenger traffic was suspended for several hours at a time to allow a single freight train full use of the 6th Street substation's output, crawling up grade from the Walla Walla River bridge with a half-dozen refrigerator cars at barely a walking pace.*
>
> *Freight interference with the passenger traffic became a moot issue in 1931, when on September 2, motorman John Wilken, who'd brought the first train into Milton, departed town with the last interurban passenger train.*[124]

The final interurban passenger train to Oregon ran on September 2, 1931. All interurban passenger service was discontinued effective October 31, 1931. Electric locomotives continued hauling freight trains until 1950, when they were replaced with diesels. Throughout those years, the freight service struggled with tracks, and an electrical supply system, that were increasingly inadequate:

> *The WWV was constructed to standards typical of rural interurban railroads. The rail was light—mostly between 56 and 72 pounds per yard. Grades were short, but exceeded two percent in several locations. And the electrical supply system, adequate for light passenger service, was completely inadequate to handle the traffic now expected of it. The railroad's four freight locomotives were all converted from trolley or interurban cars dating back to 1906. The most powerful, Motor 19, was rated at only 10 cars of prunes—440 tons—on the climb north from the Walla Walla River toward College Place. An interurban passenger car, the 322, made the switch to freight service with little outward modification, capable of hauling only three cars of prunes.*[125]

At its peak, the WWVT operated 30.90 miles of track, including city lines and sidings.[126] By the time Walla Walla's railway was abandoned by its last owner, the Burlington Northern Railroad, on May 26, 1985, its twenty-four years of passenger service and fifty-four additional years as a freight hauler had left an indelible mark in regional history. Part of that legacy was 5.51 miles of track in Oregon.

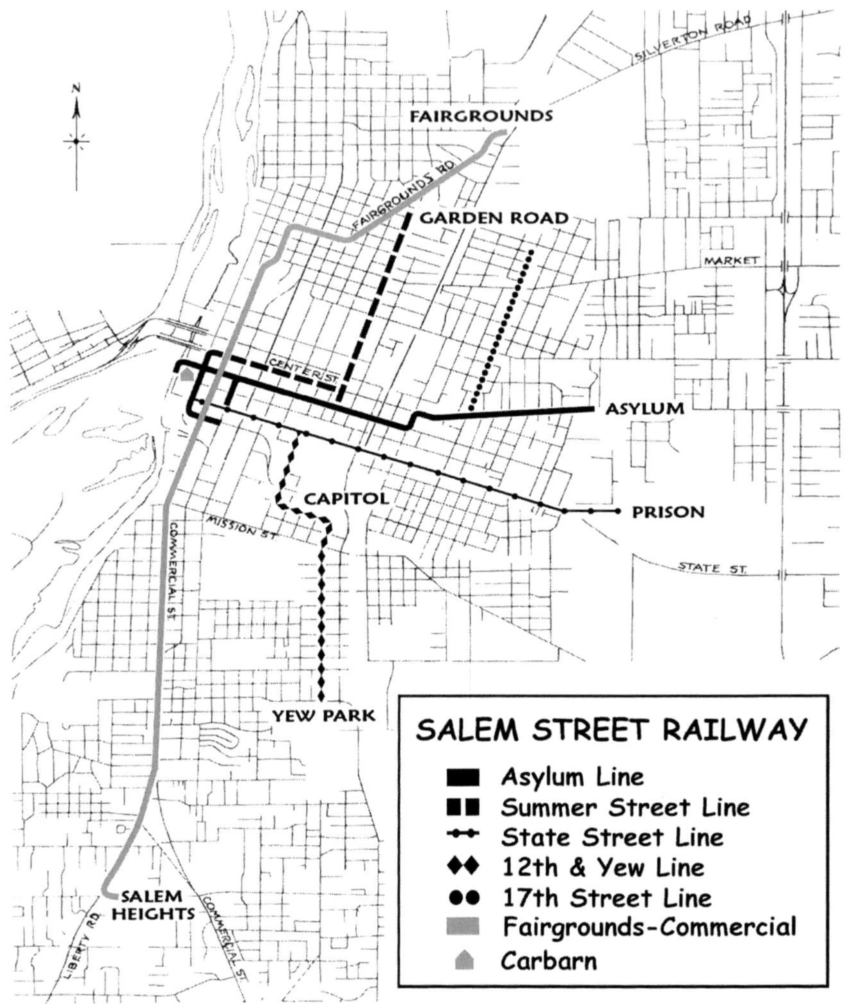

The Salem Street Railway operated six streetcar lines over about fourteen miles of track. Points throughout the east side of the Willamette River could be reached from the downtown terminus on Commercial Street. *Map modified from original by Ed Austin and Tom Dill with permission.*

Chapter 11

SALEM, 1889–1927

The Salem Street Railway began carrying passengers between the downtown business district and the train depot on January 15, 1889. The initial route was a two-and-a-half-mile horsecar line that went north on Commercial Street, east on State Street and then south on Twelfth Street to the original Oregon and California Railroad (later Southern Pacific) station. This was an important destination, since the depot had been located outside town after Salem, like other small towns, "declined" to provide the SP with a subsidy.

In December, the city's first streetcar business added branches to the Fairgrounds and to East School, bringing the system to five miles of track in total. The original franchise granted the railway the right to operate to the city limits on Center, North Commercial, Twelfth and Winter Streets. Operation was also approved on State Street west of Liberty and between Liberty and Eighteenth Streets. The company, which was headed by T.H. Hubbard, issued $20,000 in stock.

Streetcars departed every fifteen minutes during the day and every twenty minutes in the evening from a terminus at what is now 311 Commercial Street. The fare was five cents per person, and the cars were available from 6:00 a.m. until 11:00 p.m.

The Salem Street Railway's horsecars were built by the Brownell Car Company in Missouri. Service was inaugurated with two double-ended closed cars delivered from the St. Louis factory on December 27, 1889. Their ten- by six-foot closed sections accommodated sixteen passengers on

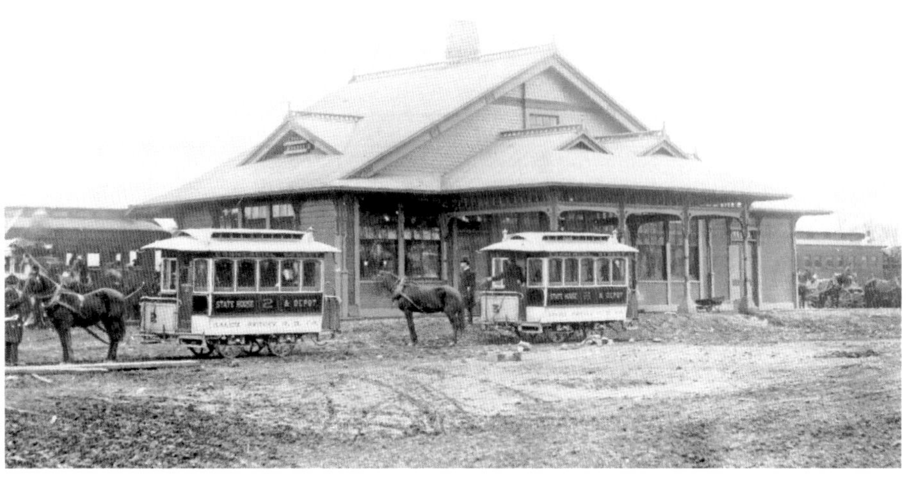

Salem Street Railway horsecars Nos. 1 and 2 await passengers outside the ornate new train depot in 1889. Note the omnibus to the left. *Courtesy Ed Austin.*

two longitudinal bench seats. The little fleet was expanded when two open "summer" cars were ordered on May 27, 1889.

A young Herbert Hoover is said to have worked part time for the streetcar company while earning money for college: "In 1889–91 Herbert Hoover, as a young boy dressed in uniform, worked as a conductor on both of these cars....Hoover's uncle, Dr. Henry J. Minthorn, was President of the Oregon Land Company which owned the horse-drawn streetcar line."[127] From 1885 until 1891, "Bert" lived with his Uncle John and Aunt Laura in Newberg. The Minthorns were administrators of the Quaker middle school (now George Fox University), which Hoover and his brother, Tad, attended. As far as this author can discover, Hoover was the only U.S. president to have experience as a carman.

In spite of mounting debt, the Salem Street Railway was able to order additional horsecars with financial assistance from Dr. Minthorn's Oregon Land Company. However, plans for an extension to Highland Addition, a real estate development being promoted by Dr. Minthorn, were put on hold in 1892, when the street railway was reorganized as the Salem Motor Railway. The electrification suggested by the new title was a belated advancement inspired by a new competitor.

On May 27, 1890, the Capital City Railway Company introduced the first electric streetcars to Salem. Salem's second streetcar enterprise, led by

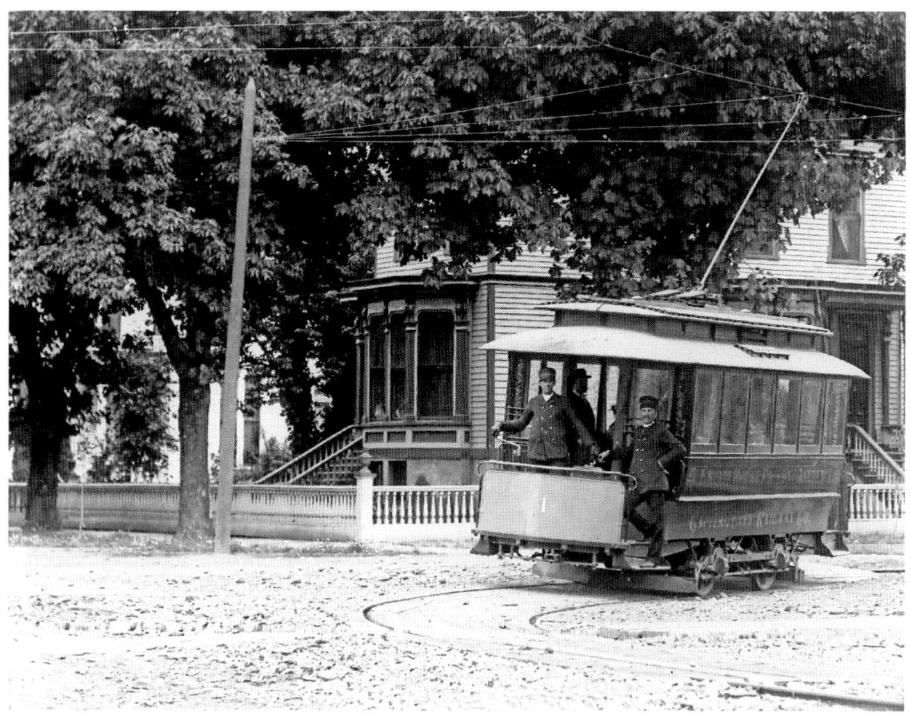

Salem's first electric streetcar posed for a picture in front of a large Italianate home on the Asylum Line circa 1891. *Courtesy Salem Oregon Public Library, Historic Photograph Collections.*

Reverend P.S. Knight and David Simpson, was launched on November 19, 1889, with $50,000 capital. Their franchise allowed for streetcar lines on Liberty, Chemeketa, State, Capitol and Court Streets and on Eighteenth Street between Chemeketa and State.

The trial run for the new electrics was on a route that began downtown, went east on Chemeketa Street to Eighteenth, south to State Street and then east again to the Penitentiary. A *Capital Journal* reporter, invited along for the two-and-a-quarter-mile ride, was awed by the mysterious energy that propelled his trolley along at an amazing speed of up to twenty-five miles per hour: "Everything moved off smoothly and all were pleased with the working of the machinery. The cars moved off rapidly and with a steady motion and there was no danger of having your neck unjoined by sudden starting and stopping."[128]

A few days later, the same reporter described a trip over the second of the initial two electric lines, which ran from downtown, south on Commercial Street, to Rural (now Pioneer) Cemetery: "He was gratified [by] the way the car walked right up Gaiety Hill with a full load and then made the 1600-foot grade beyond with a rise of 60 feet, in two minutes. May 31, 1892, was excursion day for the electric system with cars running from the penitentiary to Rural Cemetery, a distance computed as five miles, for a fare of three cents."[129]

The Capital City Railway began operation with two closed motors and two open five-bench trailers. Within three years, this fleet would grow to eleven cars. The small, single-truck trolleys had open platforms and were equipped with Edison System (General Electric) controllers and fifteen-horsepower motors. They looked very similar to horsecars and, in fact, would eventually be augmented by electrified Brownell horsecars. The trailers, at least one of which was locally manufactured by Salem Iron Works, may have been horsecars as well. A carbarn and powerhouse were erected alongside the millrace on State Street between the bridge over Mill Creek and Twenty-First Street.

Like other cities, Salem had funeral trolleys. When required, Capitol City would convert one of its open cars into a hearse. The casket would be placed on one of the wooden cross bench seats, and the pallbearers joined the family for the ride to Rural Cemetery, where they would carry the casket up the hill from Commercial Street to the grave site. An interesting side note is that the roof had to be removed from the covered bridge over Pringle Creek so that the streetcar line could be extended down Commercial Street to the cemetery.

The two railway companies continued to compete through 1894. Capital City was operating approximately seven miles of track, with lines out Chemeketa and Center Streets to the Asylum, out State Street to the Penitentiary and out Seventeenth Street to the Fairgrounds. The 1891 Fairgrounds extension, discontinued in 1894, was later reinstituted as far as Garden Road.

President E.F. Parkhurst guided the Salem Motor Railway as it converted its five miles of rail to electric operation. By 1894, five trolleys were in operation over lines running north and south along Commercial Street to the Fairgrounds and Highland Addition and out Church, Bellevue and Twelfth Streets, past the Southern Pacific Depot and then continuing on Twelfth to Yew Park.

So much track had been added during the early 1890s that Salem was thought of as having too many streetcar lines. A case in point was State Street, where competition between the two railway companies resulted in parallel tracks being laid at different grade levels—one in the middle of the road and the other along the side. All of that would change as a result of

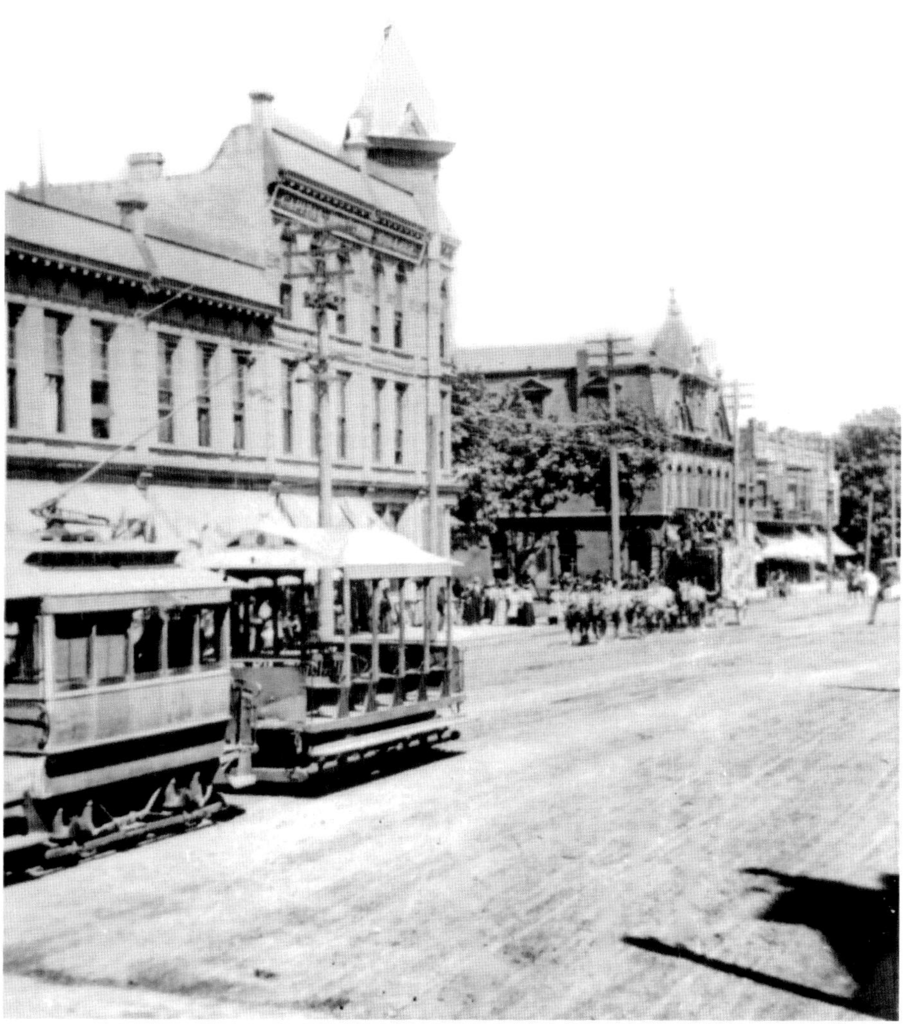

An electrified horsecar and trailer are waiting in front of Capital Business College (where future president Herbert Hoover is said to have taken classes) while a circus parade goes past. *Author's collection.*

the financial "Panic" (depression) of 1893, which brought receivership and consolidation for street railways throughout Oregon.

In 1892, the Salem Consolidated Railway Company was incorporated to, as the name implies, merge Salem's railway companies. The owner was entrepreneur George B. Markle, who was also leading a large-scale merger of street railway companies in Portland and Vancouver, Washington. Local superintendent F.R. Anson described the consolidated system as follows:

> *On November 29, F.R. Anson, agent for the Salem Electric Railway notified the public that the streetcars...would have the following routes: leave Willamette Hotel* [later the Marion] *for the Southern Pacific depot via the State House; for the Insane Asylum with a transfer to Garden Road available; and to South Salem. Cars left the Methodist Church on State Street for Morningside and the Fairgrounds. Cars operated on twenty- and thirty-minute schedules.*[130]

As things turned out, the Consolidated Railway did not last long. Like the other properties organized by George Markle and his friends, it had become a victim of the 1893 Panic. The wealthy but inexperienced Markle fled back to his Philadelphia roots, leaving the Consolidated to default on two mortgages. It was sold at a December 31, 1896 foreclosure. Superintendent F.R. Anson, who controlled most of Salem's transportation system, guided the company through receivership. The Salem Motor Railway also went through bankruptcy, emerging briefly as the Salem Suburban Railway Company.

In 1900, A.L. Barbur of Portland organized the Salem Light and Traction Company to complete the consolidation process, merging the assets of the Salem Consolidated Railway and Salem Motor Railway into a unified system that included 12.2 miles of street railway and an electric light plant. The Traction Company inherited a diverse roster that included fifteen motor streetcars and four trailers. The adept F.R. Anson continued with the new company in the multifarious capacities of general manager, purchasing agent and chief engineer.

The twentieth century brought a succession of out-of-state railway owners to Salem's transit scene. On June 11, 1904, Denver investors incorporated the Citizen's Light and Traction Company, capitalized at an impressive $200,000. Its local manager was Alvadore Welch, the electrical engineer and railway promoter who would go on to become president of the Portland, Eugene and Eastern Railway (see chapters on Albany, Eugene, West Linn and Milton-Freewater). He also appears to have retained a managerial role after Citizen's was sold to Philadelphia banking interests in September 1905.

In June 1906, Salem's streetcar system became a division of its metropolitan neighbor to the north, the Portland Railway Light and Power Company (PRL&P), which was now also owned by banking companies in Philadelphia and New York City. Between 1906 and 1911, PRL&P sent ten streetcars to Salem to replace the "antiquated" cars in use there. The late rail historian John Labbe described this influx of refurbished rolling stock:

> *The rolling stock in Salem was a hodgepodge acquired through a number of earlier mergers and dating back to the start of electric service. The old cars were a source of embarrassment to the city and of local humor to itinerant minstrels. As a gesture of goodwill Portland Railway Light & Power Company promised to equip the city with new cars. In fact, the "new" cars were discards from the Portland system that had been painted and refurbished. By December 1907 they were in service and proved a boon to riders used to the antiquated cars they replaced.*[131]

There are two sides to every issue, of course, so it is important to note that not all secondhand equipment from PRL&P was received with disdain. Interurban motors loaned to Salem in 1910 for use during the Oregon State Fair were greeted with enthusiasm (and it is interesting that the cars traveled from Portland under their own power). While the loan of those three open cars was temporary, a contemporary newspaper account also mentioned planned upgrades for cars kept in Salem:

> *The first of the new cars ordered by the Portland Railway Light & Power Co., for operation upon its lines in Salem has arrived and will be put in commission in the near future and two others are awaiting shipment in Portland and will follow up as soon as repairs to the Portland bridge are complete in order that the cars may be run to this city upon their own wheels and by their own power over the line of the Oregon Electric. This is the first step in the line of improvement in equipment and service to have been inaugurated by the company for the Salem system and the work of advancement will not stop until the service is brought up to the highest point of efficiency, equal to that of any other city on the coast.*
>
> *The new car is of the double-truck pattern, used on the Oregon City-Portland line and will fill a long felt want in the line of streetcar accommodations for the Capital City. They are equipped with double motors with a combined pulling and speed strength of 75 horse, and the interior of the cars are provided with cross seats, upholstered with*

> *bamboo cushions, and with electric heating apparatus under the seats which will keep the cars at an even and perfectly comfortable temperature during the winter months.*
>
> *The new car, which was placed upon the South Salem-Fair Grounds run for the first time yesterday afternoon, is in charge of Motorman Charles Ferrell and Conductor W.M. Busick and the patrons of the line are profuse in their expressions of satisfaction and delight in its commodious arrangement and comfortable carriage. When the other two cars arrive they will be distributed upon the several lines of the system and, will be used during state fair week as motors for the large open trailers. They will all be supplied with pneumatic air brakes.*
>
> *With three large trains of a combined carrying capacity of 450 passengers, exclusive of the present single motor equipment, the company will be prepared to handle the big fair crowds to the very best advantage and, with additional and more conveniently arranged passing tracks along the line, the running time between the city and the fair grounds will be shortened several minutes, satisfaction to all concerned. The company is also remodeling and enlarging some of the old cars of the system, and equipping them with new motors and apparatus calculated to bring the running stock up to a high standard of perfection.*[132]

Alvadore Welch began working on a planned Willamette Valley interurban railway, even as he added new streetcar lines in Salem. Construction was carried out by a number of similarly named corporations. His Eugene and Eastern Railway opened an electric streetcar system in Eugene on September 26, 1907. On December 31, 1908, the company, renamed the Portland, Eugene and Eastern Railway (PE&E), acquired the street railway in Albany. Welch's Salem, Eugene and Eastern Railway commenced work on loop tracks over Center, Front and Ferry Streets in Salem on April 22, 1910.

Two additions were made to Salem railway trackage after 1900. Around 1905, the line on South Commercial was finally extended down Liberty Road to Salem Heights. Then, on July 2, 1910, track was added from Commercial Street, east on Center Street and north on Summer Street, terminating in a field a few blocks short of Fairgrounds Road:

> *Cars were operated this afternoon on the new Welch line, known as the Salem, Eugene and Eastern system. The first car is operated every half hour between Commercial, on Center street, to the tile works near*

the fair grounds. Power is generated at the Spaulding mill plant, and regular service will be maintained in compliance with the charter. Manager F.W. Waters is to be congratulated on getting this second electric system inaugurated under the Welch management started in the Capital City.[133]

PE&E bought the city streetcar lines from PRL&P on May 5, 1912. Soon thereafter, PE&E became a subsidiary of the Southern Pacific Railroad (SP). In addition to completing much of the interurban railway envisioned by Welch, the SP was now operating city streetcars in Salem, Albany, Eugene and West Linn. The name for Salem's streetcar system was simplified under PE&E stewardship; until its demise fifteen years later, it would be known as the Salem Street Railway.

The Salem Street Railway inherited a five-track carbarn that could accommodate thirteen streetcars and eleven buses. The large reinforced-concrete facility included a machine shop, office and bus garage. It was located on the corner of Chemeketa and Front Streets, adjacent to the associated Portland Electric Power Company gas works.

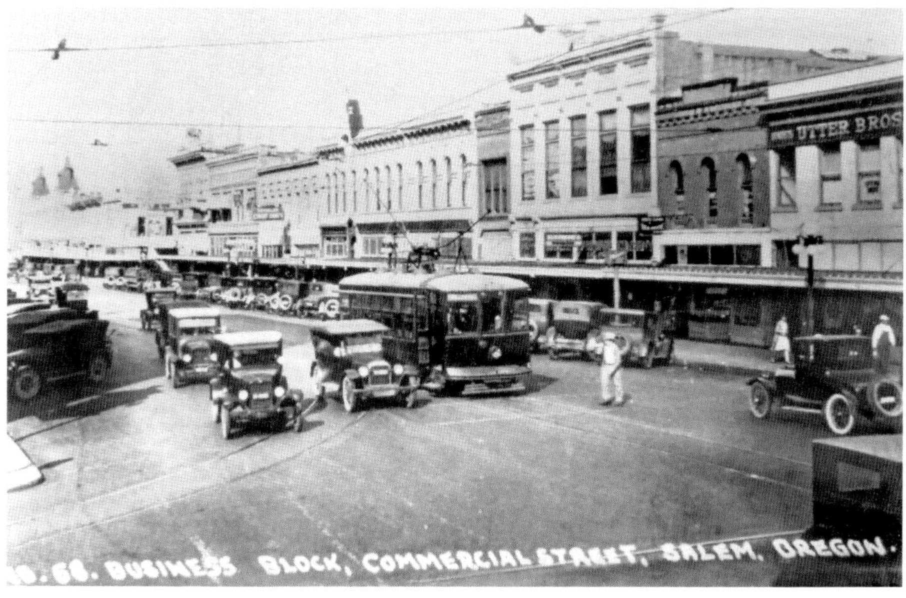

One of the Salem Street Railway's modern Birney Safety Cars is changing ends on Commercial Street at the corner of State Street in 1927, the final year for streetcar operation. *Author's collection.*

At its peak around 1913, the Salem Street Railway operated six streetcar lines over 13.8 miles of track. The network covered the entire east side of the Willamette River, radiating north, east and south to the city limits. Over the years, these lines were variously named for their destinations (Asylum, Prison, Salem Heights, State House, Y and Depot), the primary streets they ran on (A, Asylum Avenue, Chemeketa, South Commercial, State, Summer, Seventeenth and Twelfth) or a combination of both (Fairgrounds and Commercial).

In 1920, a last-ditch effort was made to reduce costs and attract ridership with the addition of new trolleys. Salem bought four Birney Safety Cars like those used in Astoria. Unfortunately, these modern streetcars were not enough to overcome losses, and they rode roughly over the deteriorated track. A newspaper story published on May 19, 1921, credited street railway superintendent T.L. Billingsley with telling a group of Marion County realtors that the city's street railways had been losing money for thirty years. He went on to say that he had been associated with the city's carlines since 1912, during which time the company had not recovered operating expenses. He pointed out that the investment in Salem's street rail transportation was $458,000 and that total loss to the operating company in 1920 had been $43,000.[134]

On November 24, 1924, the Seventeenth Street extension became the first line in which buses began replacing trolleys. The State Street Line was one of the last to be converted, on July 29, 1927. When the abandonment of all streetcar service in Salem came on August 4, 1927, the conversion to buses was made quietly:

> *No…fanfare marked the departure of Salem's street railways as acclaimed their initiation nearly 40 years before. The newspapers shed no editorial tears when Superintendent Thomas L. Billingsley announced that the trolley on East State street was coming down and that black top was covering the tracks. Bus schedules for State and Commercial streets was* [sic] *effective July 30, 1927 and on August 4, Billingsley said there was no hitch at all in the switch over from streetcars to buses.*[135]

Those backing the Salem Street Railway had been motivated as much by the desire to build lines to new real estate developments as they were by fare box revenue. They were successful in the former, reaching the Capital Home, Highland, Oaks, Simpson's and University additions, as well as Salem Heights and Yew Park. Salem's street railway became the second largest in Oregon (Eugene and Milton-Freewater had slightly more mileage, but only if you count their interurban lines). Along the way, it accumulated the widest variety of streetcar types seen in any Oregon town. At its peak, the Salem roster included nineteen cars manufactured by Brownell, Brill, Hand Manufacturing, Northern Car, Pullman, Salem Iron Works and the Stockton Combine, Harvester and Agricultural Works. Not a bad record.

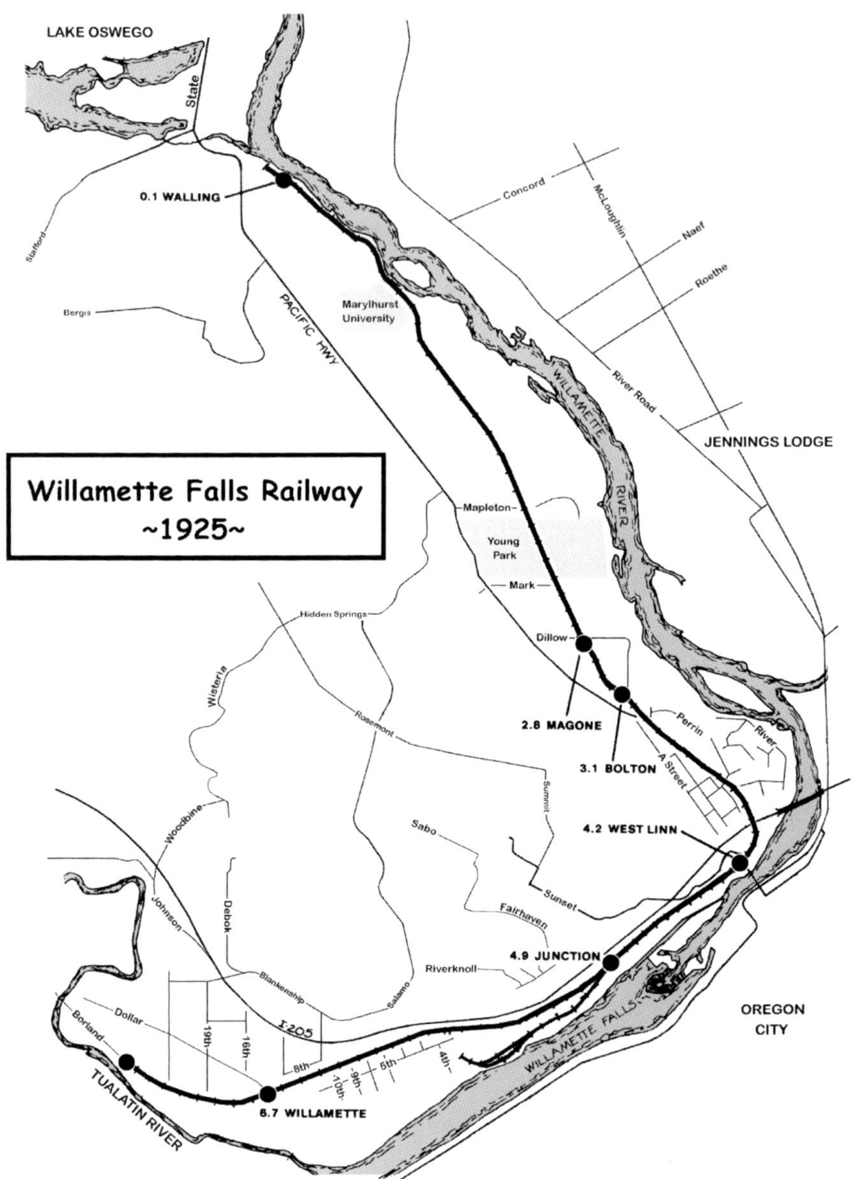

From 1894 until 1930, the Willamette Falls Railway operated passenger service over a 6.62-mile electric railway between Tualatin River Station and Walling. The northern portion of the line, between Willamette Junction and Walling, was a unique electric log-hauler that lasted three years longer (until 1933) than the passenger service. *Map modified from original by Ed Austin and Tom Dill with permission.*

Chapter 12

WEST LINN, 1894–1930

While it is true that most of Oregon's small-town streetcar systems were of limited size, and often located in areas remote from larger cities, none was more isolated than the Willamette Falls Railway (WFR), which is ironic since the line was built by a Portland General Electric Company predecessor and was only twelve miles distant from Portland. Yet in spite of attention from PRL&P and two interurban railroads, the WFR was never physically connected to any other railway. It started as what we would now call a commuter shuttle but soon gained more recognition as an electric log hauler than as a streetcar line.

On June 3, 1889, the Willamette Falls Electric Company, under the leadership of Oregon City lawyer, banker and legislator Edward Eastham, produced the nation's first long-distance transmission of electricity from four turbine-driven dynamos in the powerhouse at the Willamette Falls. This natural waterfall on the Willamette River between Oregon City and West Linn is the largest in the Northwest and the second most powerful in the United States. In the first demonstration, power harnessed from the forty-foot-high "Niagara Falls of the West" lit streetlamps in Portland, fourteen miles away.

Eastham quickly realized that alternating current, which does not lose as much power as it travels over long distances, would be more practical than the direct current originally used. So, in 1890, the company placed an order with the Westinghouse Electric Company for the largest alternators ever manufactured. An alternator is a type of generator that converts mechanical energy into electrical energy in the form of alternating current.

The Willamette Falls Electric Company was reincorporated as the Portland General Electric Company (PGE) on August 5, 1892. Three years later, the oldest power plant west of the Mississippi River, Station A on the Oregon City side of the Falls, was replaced by Station B on the opposite shore in West Linn (then known as Linn City). Among the first businesses to take advantage of the new source of electric power was the East Side Railway, which completed the nation's first interurban railway, between Oregon City and Portland, in 1893. Soon there would be an electric railway in Willamette Falls as well. Both companies were supplied with energy from the dam located alongside the old locks that had opened to navigation on January 1, 1873.

Edward Eastham and his associates created several similarly named subsidiary companies to raise capital. In 1893, one of these, the Willamette Falls Development Company, platted a seventeen-block town site on a ridge running along the west side of the Willamette River across from Oregon City. Real estate speculator Nicholas Walden led the development company as construction started on what was intended to be an industrial town with a river port. To attract residents and business, the developer promised the latest urban amenities, including electric lights, running water, sewers and a streetcar line. Unfortunately, Walden passed away in 1897, and the idea for a modern port city perished along with him. While a small business district developed along Seventh Avenue, sales of lots for new homes slowed, and industrial expansion yielded to competition from Oregon City.

Several plats, clustered near the west end of the Oregon City bridge, were developed between 1889 and 1896. These included the West Side Addition, Windsor, Wesylnn, Sunset, Parker Hill, Willamette Falls and Bolton. All were predominantly residential, except for Willamette Falls, which developed as a complete community.

The relationship of PGE to the Willamette Falls Development Company and its electric railway line was set out in a public utilities report:

> *Willamette Falls Development Company: No records of this company are available, but it appears on September 14, 1893, the fixed assets were transferred to the Willamette Falls Company in consideration of the issuance to the Portland General Electric Company of $90,500 of Willamette Falls Company stock. This transfer was apparently made in consideration of advances made by the Portland General Electric Company to the Willamette Falls Development Company.*

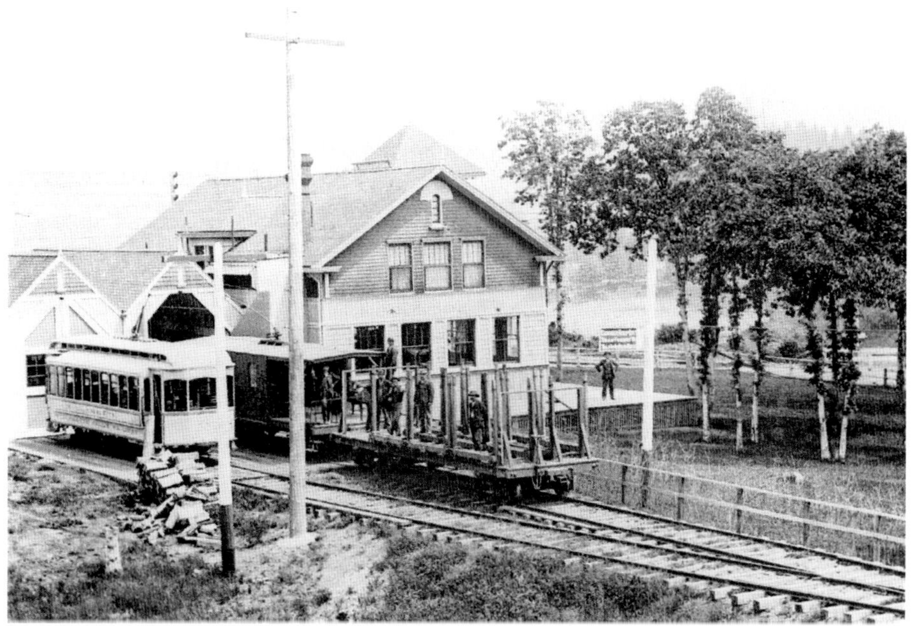

The interurban car "Willamette," a locally built box motor, and a log car sit on the ladder track next to the West Linn depot in about 1910. The unique depot also housed the West Linn City Hall. *Author's collection.*

> *Willamette Falls Company* [was] *incorporated in 1893, with a capital stock of $100,000, this company issued $99,500 of its stock to the Portland General Electric Company as above, taking over the assets of the Willamette Falls Development Company. The remainder of the stock was issued to the Portland General Electric Company on September 26, 1898, and on January 17, 1907, that company took over a line of electric railway, owned by this company, near Oregon City.*[136]

In early 1893, the Willamette Falls Development Company (now the Willamette Falls Company) began construction of an electric railway. Originally conceived as a means to promote real estate development, the line would provide an important service by transporting employees to Willamette Falls' (later simplified to Willamette) only industry, the Capen Shoe Factory; to the power station then under construction in West Linn; and to the Willamette Pulp and Paper mill in Bolton. A two-bay carbarn and a handsome shingle-sided station were erected in West Linn. Until it was demolished in 1936, the station held the unique distinction of also serving as the city hall.

In July 1893, ownership of the new streetcar line was transferred to the Willamette Falls Railway (WFR). The original three-mile route from the town of Willamette Falls to the powerhouse in Linn City opened in February 1894. Two new streetcars, ordered from the J.G. Brill Company in Philadelphia, had not arrived in time to inaugurate service, so that role fell to a car borrowed from the East Side Railway Company. Since the East Side Railway's tracks were on the opposite side of the Willamette River, the interurban trolley had to be hauled across the suspension bridge from Oregon City on temporary tracks.

The railway's isolated location kept fare box revenue low, but it developed a brisk business as a lumber carrier. In April 1894, a locally built electric locomotive began hauling cordwood cut along the Tualatin River to the Willamette Pulp and Paper mill. Trains of log cars were soon hauling one hundred cords of wood per day. By 1900, the demand for wood prompted construction of a freight extension across the Tualatin River to a point approximately one and a half miles from the town of Willamette. This was before the era of trees being harvested as a crop, however, so when the wood in this area was depleted, the railway extension was abandoned.

The WFR played a role in the consolidation of the towns along its route. In 1908, Willamette became the first to incorporate as a city. When West Linn followed suit in 1913, it merged the communities of West Oregon City, Bolton, Sunset and Willamette Heights. Finally, in 1916, Willamette and West Linn were joined.

In 1906, eastern investors merged the Portland Railway Company, PGE and Oregon Water Power and Railway Company to form the Portland Railway, Light and Power Company (PRL&P). This conglomerate brought together power generation facilities, street railways and interurban railways throughout Portland and much of the Willamette Valley. On January 17, 1907, the WFR became a subsidiary of PRL&P.

At first, the corporate giant seems to have been uncertain of what to do with the little WFR. After the merger, it was assigned to the Oregon City Division of PGE. However, the lines operated directly by the electric utility were used for moving fuel (sawdust) around power-generating stations, not hauling passengers. So, on January 31, 1907, the WFR was transferred to the Portland Railway Division of PRL&P.

PGE no doubt hoped that the WFR would encourage development of its extensive holdings on the west bank of the Willamette River. Indeed, by 1908 it had joined other large corporations in platting additional residential neighborhoods around West Linn.

In May 1909, PRL&P announced a grand plan to extend the WFR northward to Lake Oswego and then across the Willamette River, where it would connect with a planned interurban railroad heading south to Molalla and beyond:

> *This company (PRL&P) announces that work will begin soon on a 4-mile branch from West Oregon City to Oswego. It will be an extension of the Willamette Falls Railway running south from West Oregon City past Willamette. It is reported that the company will build a bridge across the Willamette at Rock Island and build an electric railway into the New Era, Molalla and Marquam country.*[137]

A move in this direction was made in April 1914 when PRL&P bought the Willamette Valley Southern Railway, which was building south from Oregon City, through Molalla, to Mount Angel. That 31.9-mile route opened on October 23, 1915; however, a railway bridge across the Willamette River at Rock Island was never constructed, nor was the WFR extended to Lake Oswego.

It was also thought that a WFR branch might connect with the Oregon Electric Railway, which was building an interurban from Portland to Eugene. Had such a junction been made, it would have increased the value of the WFR to potential buyers. It should be noted, however, that it was actually the rival Southern Pacific Railroad that would eventually purchase the WFR:

> *C.A. Miller, of the Portland Railway, Light & Power Co., has been ordered to start surveys for the construction of an electric railway from Oregon City, Ore. to Oswego, on the west side of the Willamette River. The road will connect with the Willamette Falls R.R. running from Oregon City to Willamette Falls and on to Tualatin River and probably to a connection with the Oregon Electric at some point.*[138]

Grandiose interurban connections aside, a northern branch of the WFR to Lake Oswego was also inspired by a need for logs by local pulp and paper mills, as can be seen in this 1910 report from a contractor's magazine:

> *The Portland Railway, Light and Power Company of Portland has completed surveys for the construction of an electric railway from West Oregon City to Oswego, a distance of four miles, in order to handle the logging business for Willamette Pulp & Paper Co., the Crown-Columbia*

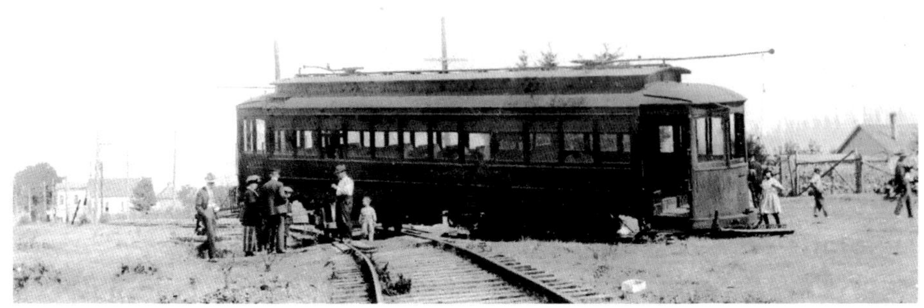

The children seem to be enjoying the occasion as a derailed Willamette Falls Railway Brill trolley awaits assistance, circa 1916. *Courtesy Donald R. Nelson.*

> *Pulp & Paper Co., and the Hawley Pulp & Paper Co. The line will be an extension of the Willamette Falls Railway running south from West Oregon City past Willamette, and the surveys were made by Superintendent C.A. Miller of the Willamette Falls Co. It is intended to have the road in operation within three months.*[139]

A half-mile northern extension, to Magone, was built in 1911. The addition, while short, was productive, because it gave the WFR a recreational destination. Magone Station was a short walk from Magone's Park on the shore of the Willamette River. This pleasure park may not have featured fancy rides like those at the Oaks, a few miles downstream in Sellwood, but its rental cottages, food, swimming and rowboats were locally popular. Even better, the dancing barge *Bluebird* was anchored off the beach.

WFR passengers could ride to a fine hotel as well. In 1918, Willamette Pulp and Paper Company successor Crown Zellerbach Corporation built a workers' dormitory in Bolton. Legend has it that the original tenants were strikebreakers brought in to prevent an effort by mill employees to unionize. Nevertheless, as the town of West Linn grew and workers moved into their own homes, the dormitory evolved into the West Linn Inn. This eighty-five-room hotel was known for its long veranda overlooking Willamette Falls, marble-floored lobby with a huge stone fireplace and basement bowling alley.

On November 8, 1912, the Portland, Eugene and Eastern Railway (PE&E) bought the WFR. PE&E had become a subsidiary of the Southern Pacific Railroad (SP), which was seeking a route along the west bank of the Willamette River for its electrified Red Electric interurban line from Portland to Eugene. The SP was interested in using part of the WFR right-of-way for its interurban, and there was talk of relocating the Red Electric shops to West Linn.

The nationwide interurban-building boom was still in full swing at this point, so surveys were made for a mainline through Oswego, West Linn, Hubbard, Independence and Salem. The new route would have required replacement, or realignment, of much WFR track. As it turned out, none of these things happened. Instead, the Red Electric electrification turned west at Lake Oswego, toward Tualatin, leaving the WFR as an isolated segment of the mighty SP.

The PE&E's plans for the WFR were described in a 1913 trade publication:

> *In carrying out its scheme for the electrification of the Willamette Valley and the establishment of a suburban service of the utmost importance to Portland business interests, the Portland, Eugene & Eastern Railway Company has purchased from the Portland Railway, Light & Power Company, of Portland, Ore. the nine-mile stretch of railway track known as the Willamette Falls Railway, and in part will utilize the old road as a portion of the new main line from Portland to Salem. Contracts are now being let by R.T. Guppy. chief engineer, for a large portion of the main line grade between Portland and Salem, and it is expected that the work will be prosecuted during the entire rainy season. Twenty miles of the north end of the grade are to be constructed for a double track system which is intended to afford facilities for all interurban trains to reach Portland on time by avoiding congestion after the various roads through the valley deliver their trains to the main line. The Willamette Falls Railway which built the road in 1891 was a subsidiary company of the Portland General Electric. It was intended to develop the town of Willamette Falls, where many of the workmen from the pulp mills made their homes, but of late years has been engaged in carrying innumerable cords of wood to the mills.*[140]

After the PE&E bought the WFR, improvements were made to its unique freight-hauling capability. In 1914, the line was extended from Magone to Walling, near Lake Oswego, and a spur was built to a log dump just above the Willamette Falls. It was positioned so that the railway could move logs around the falls. In a rather inefficient procedure, SP trains on the Tillamook branch would dump logs into the river at Menefee, where they could be rafted upriver to the reload at Walling. They were then lifted out of the river and placed on flatcars. When four flatcars had been loaded, electric steeplecab locomotives would haul them to a log dump below Junction. Here they were dumped back into the river and rafted back downstream to the Willamette Pulp and Paper Company mill in West Linn.

On July 1, 1915, all properties of the PE&E—including streetcar systems in Albany, Eugene, Salem and West Linn—were officially transferred to the Southern Pacific Railroad. That year, a new steeplecab locomotive, No. 100, arrived to help handle WFR log trains. Three electric locomotives would eventually be assigned to SP's log-hauling railway.

At the height of its operation, the WFR grew to encompass nearly 9 miles of track. During the 1920s, after logging branch cutbacks, total mileage was 6.65.[141] With logs providing most of the traffic, the SP focused on what was known as the "Wood Train," while independent crews operated two streetcars over the 3.9-mile southern portion of the line. Both operations shared trackage in the middle, between Magone and Willamette Junction. Passenger service was provided between the stations of Tualatin River and Magone, with stops at Willamette Junction, West Linn and Bolton. The 1925 timetable shows streetcars making sixty-two trips per day, between the hours of 6:05 a.m. and 12:53 a.m.

The WFR operated with five different streetcars over the years, although only three or four were present at the same time. Two double-truck streetcars were ordered from J.G. Brill's Philadelphia plant in 1893, but when they were delayed at the factory, passenger service began with an interurban borrowed from the East Side Railway. The first new car arrived in March 1894, painted in a bright cream and bearing the name "Willamette" (an attractive color scheme that was difficult to maintain, since the Brills were soon wearing darker livery). Three more streetcars were added during the PE&E years. No. 11 was leased from PRL&P around 1913, and in 1915, long suburban Niles car No. 10 was transferred from Eugene-Springfield service. The final passenger car to join the roster was PRL&P's obsolescent Holman-built interurban No. 1035, which replaced No. 11 in 1917. The last WFR streetcar was retired in May 1930.

Surviving records suggest that the WFR roster included three electric locomotives over the years. The first locomotive, an 1894 locally built effort, was later augmented by electric steeplecab locomotives from the SP. The only one of these seen in photographs was former PE&E No. 100, a 1912

Baldwin-Westinghouse product. No. 100 was sold to other railroads after retirement in early 1933.

The streetcar line dubbed Oregon's most obscure began to fade in the late 1920s, as automobiles became common. Streetcar service on the WFR was reduced in 1927, when buses began to operate between Willamette, Bolton and Oregon City. The remaining streetcar service was discontinued in 1930. Three years later, the logging railroad ceased.

Appendix

TABLES

Table 1. Oregon's Lost Streetcars

Albany

No.	*Builder*	*Built*	*Type*	*Trk.*	*Mtr.*	*Pass.*	*Ret.*	*Remarks*
1	Albany Iron Works	1889	Horse	1, Albany Iron	N/A	12	1909	
?			Horse					Larger
3	Baldwin	1892	Dummy	2-4-0T	N/A		1895	
1 (2nd)	Porter	1891	Dinky	0-4-2T	N/A		1900	Wheels changed, to Skelly 1905
1 (3rd)	J.G. Brill	1906	Semi-con.	2, Brill 27	2, GE-87A	32	1928	Rebuilt to one-man PAYE '16
2	J.G. Brill	1907	Semi-con.	2, Brill 27	2 GE-87A	32	1928	Rebuilt to one-man PAYE '16
3 (2nd)	J.G. Brill	1907	Semi-con.	2 Brill 27	2 GE-87A	32	1928	Rebuilt to one-man PAYE '16

No.	Builder	Built	Type	Trk.	Mtr.	Pass.	Ret.	Remarks
70	Danville Car Co.	1910	Semi-con.	1, Brill 21E	2 GE-87A	32	1928	Rebuilt to one-man PAYE '16
76	St. Louis Car Co.	1909	Calif.	2	West101B-2	48	1927	PE 217
77	St. Louis Car Co.	1909	Calif.	2	West101B-2	48	1927	PE 215
78	St. Louis Car Co.	1909	Calif.	2	West101B-2	48	1927	PE 216

Astoria

No.	Builder	Built	Type	Trk.	Mtr.	Pass.	Ret.	Remarks
1	Brownell	1888	Horse	1	N/A	12		
1	Baldwin	1890	Dummy	0-4-0	N/A	N/A	1895	
2	Brownell	1888	Horse	1	N/A	12		
3	Brownell	1888	Horse, elect. 1891	1 Brill	2	12		Enlarged to 30 ft. 1896
4	Brownell	1889	Horse, elect. 1891	1 Brill	2	12		
5	Brownell	1888	Open horse	1	N/A			Later used as trailer
6	Brownell	1888	Open horse	1	N/A			Later used as trailer
7	Brownell	1889	Horse, elect. 1891	1 Brill	2	12		Enlarged to 30 ft. 1896
8	Brownell	1889	Horse, elect. 1891	1 Brill	2	12		Enlarged to 30 ft. 1896
3 (2nd)		1901	9-window Bombay roof	1	2			
4 (2nd)		1901	9-window Bombay roof	1	2			

No.	Builder	Built	Type	Trk.	Mtr.	Pass.	Ret.	Remarks
5 (2nd)		1901	9-window Bombay roof	1	2		1924	
6 (2nd)	American	1903	Semi-convert.	1, Brill 21E	2			
7 (2nd)	American	1907	Semi-convert.	1, Brill 21E	2		1924	
8 (2nd)	American	1907	Semi-convert.	1, Brill 21E	2		1924	
9	American	1907	Semi-convert.	1, Brill 21E	2			
10	American	1913	Semi-convert.	1, Brill Radiax	2			28 feet
11	American	1913	Semi-convert.	1, Brill Radiax	2			28 feet
12	American	1913	Semi-convert.	1, Brill Radiax	2			28 feet
14	American	1914	PAYE	1, long Radiax			1924	34 feet
15	American	1918	Birney	1, Brill 21E	2, GE-258C		1924	28 feet
16	American	1920	Birney	1, Brill 79E	2, GE-258C		1924	28 feet

Baker City

No.	Builder	Built	Type	Trk.	Mtr.	Pass.	Ret.	Remarks
1?		1890	Horse	1	N/A	12		2–3 cars?
2		1890	Horse	1	N/A	12	1902	

Cherry Grove

No.	Builder	Built	Type	Trk.	Mtr.	Pass.	Ret.	Remarks
	Mitchell	?	Autocar	N/A		7	1912	Converted auto

No.	Builder	Built	Type	Trk.	Mtr.	Pass.	Ret.	Remarks
10	Federal Storage Battery	1911	Battery	2, fixed axle	4 GE 5 hp	45	1928	"Goose," 28 feet
1		c. 1929	Gasoline railcar				1934	"Skunk"

Corvallis

No.	Builder	Built	Type	Trk.	Mtr.	Pass.	Ret.	Remarks
1?		1890	Horse	1	N/A	12	1896	"Daisy"
2		1890	Horse	1	N/A	12	1896	

Eugene

No.	Builder	Built	Type	Trk.	Mtr.	Pass.	Ret.	Remarks
1	Pullman?	1891	Mule	1	N/A		1900	To Salem
2	Pullman?	1891	Mule	1	N/A		1900	To Salem
3	Pullman?	1891	Mule	1	N/A		1900	To Salem
4	Pullman?	1891	Mule	1	N/A		1900	To Salem
1 (2nd)	J.G. Brill	1906	Semi-convert.	2, Brill 27	2, GE-87A	32	1928	PAYE 1916, SP 850
2 (2nd)	J.G. Brill	1907	Semi-convert.	2, Brill 27	2, GE-87A	36	1928	PAYE 1916, SP 851
3 (2nd)	J.G. Brill	1907	Semi-convert.	2, Brill 27	2, GE-87A	32	1928	PAYE 1916, SP 852
4 (2nd)	J.G. Brill	1906	Open	2	2, Allis-Chalmers	72	1913	SP 859, to tower car 0202, wreck '21
6	J.G. Brill	1908	Semi-convert.	2	2, GE-52A	40	1916	
7	J.G. Brill	1908	Semi-convert.	2	2, GE-52A	40	1921	SP 875
8	J.G. Brill	1906	Semi-convert.	2	2, GE-52A	40	1922	SP 876

No.	*Builder*	*Built*	*Type*	*Trk.*	*Mtr.*	*Pass.*	*Ret.*	*Remarks*
9	J.G. Brill	1907		2, Brill C1	2, GE-87A	36	1928	Rebuilt to PAYE '16 SP 853
10	Niles		Suburban	2	2, GE-216E	48	1915 to West Linn	From Centralia 1912, SP 860
11	J.G. Brill		Suburban	2	2, GE-67A	40	1917 to West Linn	From PRL&P 1913
11 (2nd)	St. Louis Car Co.	1909	Calif.	2	2, WH No. 101B-2	48	1927	Ex PE 218, to SP 857
12	St. Louis Car Co.	1909	Calif.	2	2, WH No. 101B-2	48	1927	Ex PE 219, to SP 858
76	St. Louis Car Co.	1909	Calif.	2	2, WH No. 101B-2	48	1927	Ex PE 217, to SP 856
77	St. Louis Car Co.	1909	Calif.	2	2, WH No. 101B-2	48	1927	Ex PE 215, to SP 854
78	St. Louis Car Co.	1909	Calif.	2	2, WH No. 101B-2	48	1927	Ex PE 216, to SP 855
917	American Car Co.	1914	Near Side	2, Brill 39E	2, GE-216E	36	1928	SP 867
918	American Car Co.	1914	Near Side	2, Brill 39E	2, GE-216E	36	1928	SP 868
919	American Car Co.	1914	Near Side	2, Brill 39E	2, GE-216E	36	1928	SP 869
920	American Car Co.	1914	Near Side	2, Brill 39E	2, GE-216E	36	1928	SP 870

Forest Grove

No.	Builder	Built	Type	Trk.	Mtr.	Pass.	Ret.	Remarks
None	Brownell	1890	Inter-urban	2			1911	Electrified trailer

Klamath Falls

No.	Builder	Built	Type	Trk.	Mtr.	Pass.	Ret.	Remarks
?	Sutter St. Railway	1870s	Horse	1	N/A		1910	

Medford and Jacksonville

No.	Builder	Built	Type	Trk.	Mtr.	Pass.	Ret.	Remarks
1	St. Louis Car Co.	1914	Birney	1, Brill 21E	2, GE	34	1920	
2	St. Louis Car Co.	1915	Birney	1, Brill	2, GE	34	1920	
220	Kuhlman	1902	Suburb-an	2		56	1920	Orig. single ended
1	Porter	1891	Dinky	2-4-0T	N/A	N/A	1895	To Albany, where modified
1 (2nd)	Fairbanks	1905	Gasoline railcar	N/A	FB-Morse 2 Cyl.	7	1916	To Butte Falls
2	Ferry Garage	1909	Railcar		Brennan 4 Cyl.	22	1916	To Butte Falls

Milton and Freewater

No.	Builder	Built	Type	Trk.	Mtr.	Pass.	Ret.	Remarks
2	J.G. Brill	1906	Combine, 31 ft.	2, Brill 27-G1	GE			Passenger & express baggage

No.	*Builder*	*Built*	*Type*	*Trk.*	*Mtr.*	*Pass.*	*Ret.*	*Remarks*
	J.G. Brill	1906	Combine, 31 ft.	2, Brill 27-G1	GE			Passenger & express baggage
7			open trailer			60		12-bench
8			open trailer			60		12-bench
19	American Car Co.		Inter-urban	19				
21	American Car Co.	1908	Combine, 46 ft.	2, Brill 27-E1	2, GE	53	1931	Smoking section
22	American Car Co.	1908	Combine, 46 ft.	2, Brill 27-E1	2, GE	53	1931	Smoking section

Salem

No.	*Builder*	*Built*	*Type*	*Trk.*	*Mtr.*	*Pa.*	*Ret.*	*Remarks*
1	Brownell	1889	Horse	1	N/A	16		
2	Brownell	1889	Horse	1	N/A	16		
	Salem Iron Works	1889	Open horse	1	N/A	SIW		
		1889	Open horse					
	Pullman?	1891	Horse	1	N/A		1900	Ex-Eugene
	Pullman?	1891	Horse	1	N/A		1900	Ex-Eugene
	Pullman?	1891	Horse	1	N/A		1900	Ex-Eugene
	Pullman?	1891	Horse	1	N/A		1900	Ex-Eugene
1	Pullman?	1890	Motor	1	2 GE			
2	Pullman?	1890	Motor	1	2 GE			
		1890	Open trailer	1	N/A			5-bench, same as above?
		1890	Open trailer	1	N/A			5-bench, same as above?

No.	*Builder*	*Built*	*Type*	*Trk.*	*Mtr.*	*Pa.*	*Ret.*	*Remarks*
4			Calif.	2				
8			Calif.	2				
30	J.G. Brill							
36	Hand Mfg.?	1893	Motor	1, Dupont				
40	Hand Mfg?	1893	Motor	1, Dupont				
44	J.G. Brill		Open	1, Dupont	2, GE-800B	40	1919	7-bench, wrecked SP 877
46	Hand Mfg.	1893	Motor	1, Dupont	2, GE-800B	28		SP 878
48?	J.G. Brill		Open	1, Dupont	2, GE-800B			7-bench
52	Hand Mfg.	1893	Motor	1, Dupont	2, GE-800B	28	1916	
54	Northern Car Co.	c. 1893	Interurban	2, OWP	2, GE-67A	32	1920	OWP 39, PRL&P 1039, SP 871, wrecked
56	Northern Car Co.	c. 1893	Interurban	2, OWP	2, Stanley 401	32	1927	OWP 40, PRL&P 1040, SP 872
58	Northern Car Co.	c. 1893	Interurban	2, OWP	2, GE-67A	32	1927	OWP 41, PRL&P 1041, SP 873
60	J.G. Brill		Open	1, Dupont	2, GE-800B		1916	7-bench
61	Hand Mfg.	1893	Motor	1, Dupont	2, GE-800B	28		SP 879
70	Danville Car Co.	1910	Motor	1, Brill-21E	2, GE-216E	34	1927	PAYE 1916, SP 861
71	Danville Car Co.	1910	Motor	1, Brill-21E	2, GE-216E	34	1927	PAYE 1916, SP 862

No.	*Builder*	*Built*	*Type*	*Trk.*	*Mtr.*	*Pa.*	*Ret.*	*Remarks*
72	Danville Car Co.	1910	Motor	1, Brill-21E	2, GE-216E	34	1927	PAYE 1916, SP 863
73	Danville Car Co.	1910	Motor	1, Brill-21E	2, GE-216E	34	1927	PAYE 1916, SP 864
74	Danville Car Co.	1910	Motor	1, Brill-21E	2, GE-216E	34	1927	
75	Danville Car Co.	1910	Motor	1, Brill-21E	2, GE-216E	34	1927	PAYE 1916, SP 866
880	J.G. Brill	1920	Bir-ney	1, Brill-79E	2, GE-258C	36	1927	Double end, One man
881	J.G. Brill	1920	Bir-ney	1, Brill-79E	2, GE-258C	36	1927	Double end, One man
882	J.G. Brill	1920	Birney	1, Brill-79E	2, GE-258C	36	1927	Double end, One man
883	J.G. Brill	1920	Birney	1, Brill-79E	2, GE-258C	36	1927	Double end, One man
1035	Holman	1901	Inter-urban, 39.5 ft.	2 OWP	2, GE-57	40	1927	OWP 35, SP 874
1037	Northern/ Indianapolis Car Co.	1892	Interurban, 38 ft.	2-OWP	2, GE-57	40		To Salem 1911, to PRL&P 1914

West Linn

No.	*Builder*	*Built*	*Type*	*Trk.*	*Mtr.*	*Pass.*	*Ret.*	*Remarks*
?	J.G. Brill	1893	Interurban	2				"Willamette"?
	J.G. Brill	1893	Interurban					
10	Niles	1912	Suburban	2	2, GE-216E	48	1930	From Eugene 1915, SP 860

No.	*Builder*	*Built*	*Type*	*Trk.*	*Mtr.*	*Pass.*	*Ret.*	*Remarks*
11	J.G. Brill	1913		1	2, GE-67A	40	1917	From PRL&P, 1913 to 1917.
1035	Holman	1901	Interurban	2, OWP	2, GE-57	40	1930	From PRL&P, replaced No. 11

Key

American	American Car Company, St. Louis, MO (became Brill subsidiary 1902)
Brownell	Brownell Car Company, St. Louis, MO
Calif.	California-style streetcar (part open, part closed)
Danville	Danville Car Company, Danville, IL (became Brill subsidiary 1908)
Hand Mfg.	Hand Manufacturing Company, Portland, OR
Holman	W.L. Holman Company, San Francisco, CA
Indianapolis	Indianapolis Car and Manufacturing Company, Indianapolis, IN
J.G. Brill	J.G. Brill Company, Philadelphia, PA
Kuhlman	G.C. Kuhlman Car Company, Cleveland, OH (became Brill subsidiary 1904)
Mtr.	Motors
Niles	Niles Car and Manufacturing Company, Niles, OH
Northern	Northern Car Company, Chicago, IL, and Minneapolis, MN
Pass.	passenger capacity (seated)
Porter	H.K. Porter and Company, Pittsburgh, PA
Pullman	Pullman Palace Car Company, Pullman, IL
Ret.	retired date
Salem Iron Wrks	Salem Iron Works, Salem, OR
Semi-convert.	semi-convertible
Trk	trucks (sets of wheels, 1 = 4, 2 = 8)

Note: This roster includes only those streetcars found in old photographs or specifically mentioned in earlier works. Works consulted included the correspondence of David L. Stearns and John Labbe, a chart submitted by Mitch Mitchum, the roster in *The Red Electrics: Southern Pacific's Oregon Interurban* (see bibliography) and *Interurbans Special Number 8: The Red Electrics of Portland*. Although incomplete, it presents as comprehensive a record of Oregon's small-town streetcars as possible. It is hoped that feedback from readers will help fill in the blanks.

TABLE 2. SMALL-TOWN STREETCAR SYSTEMS

City	*Opened*	*Ceased*	*Years*	*Cars*	*Lines*	*Miles*	*Last*
Albany	August 30, 1889	1918	29	2H, 1D, 1S, 1C, 7M	2	1.5	1910
Astoria	May 9, 1888	June 30, 1924	36	6H, 2T, 1D, 3O, 17M	2	5.7	1920
Baker City	June 4, 1890	circa 1904	14	2H	1	1.1	1890
Cherry Grove	June 30, 1912	1933	11	1B, 2R, 1C, 1S	1	5.8	1928
Corvallis	June 19, 1890	circa 1896	6	2H	1	2	1890
Eugene	June 26, 1891	October 15, 1927	32*	4H, 18M, 1O	4	18	1912
Forest Grove	May, 1906	1911	5	1I	1	1.7	1906
Jacksonville	February 18, 1891**	April 1, 1925***	34	3M, 2R, 1C, 3S	1	6	1916
Klamath Falls	July 4, 1907	May 9, 1911	3	1H	1	3.5	1907
Medford	March 20, 1914	1922	8	3M	1	2.5	1916
Milton and Freewater	April 17, 1907	September 2, 1931	24	4I, 2O	1	14 (5.5)	1908
Salem	January 15, 1889	August 4, 1927	38	6H, 18M, 5O, 5I	6	13.8	1920
West Linn	February 1894	May 1930	37	3I, 2M	1	9	1917

Key to Car Types
B = battery car, C = railroad coach, D = dummy, H = horsecar, I = interurban, M = closed motor, O = open car, S = steam locomotive, R = self-propelled railcar

Notes: Streetcars listed are totals, not cars in use at the same time; "Last" column indicates the last new car order.

*four-year gap with no system
** began as steam short line (not electrified until 1916)
*** steam locomotive, freight only at end (no electric)

NOTES

Chapter 1

1. *Albany Democrat*, August, 1889.
2. Mullen, *Land of Linn*, 134–35.
3. *Oregonian*, June 5, 1912.
4. *Oregonian*, September 3, 1912.
5. *Oregonian*, October 22, 1906.
6. *Oregonian*, March 9, 1908.
7. *Oregonian*, May 12, 1911.
8. *Oregonian*, February 24, 1911.
9. Ibid.
10. *Oregonian*, March 13, 1914.
11. *Oregonian*, August 12, 1917.

Chapter 2

12. *Oregonian*, January 29, 1890.
13. Ibid., February 1, 1890.
14. Ibid., February 13, 1890.
15. Ibid., January 26, 1890.
16. Ibid., March 12, 1890.
17. Ibid., May 16, 1890.
18. Ibid., May 20, 1890.

19. Ibid., June 23, 1890.
20. *Daily Astorian*, November 24, 1889.
21. *Oregonian*, January 23, 1890.
22. Ibid., September 21, 1891.
23. *Daily Astorian*, November 17, 1891.
24. Ibid., February 11, 1893.
25. *Street Railway Journal* (May 1893): 317.
26. Ibid. (December 7, 1907): 1,118.
27. *McGraw Electric Railway Directory*, 1924, 141.
28. *Oregonian*, December 9, 1922.
29. Astoria Riverfront Trolley, http://www.old300.org/history.

Chapter 3

30. *Street Railway Journal* 5 (1889): 162.
31. Ibid.
32. Pearl Jones, "Horse Trolley," *Baker City Herald*, April 23, 2006.
33. *Electrical World* 16 (August 2, 1890): 79.
34. *Poor's Directory of Railway Officials*, 1893, 258.
35. *Sunday Oregonian*, June 4, 1899, 10.
36. Debby Schoeningh, "Rock Creek Power Plant—Once a Source of Power—Now a Source of History," Oregon Genealogy, oregongenealogy.com.
37. *Sunday Oregonian*, January 10, 1904, 5.
38. *Morning Oregonian*, April 27, 1907.
39. *Electric Railway Journal* 33, no. 25 (1909): 1,146.
40. Ibid. (September 11, 1909).

Chapter 4

41. McArthur, *Oregon Geographic Names*, 151.
42. Brian McCamish, Active and Abandoned Railroads of the Pacific Northwest, http://www.brian894x4.com/WillametteValleyandCoastRR.html.
43. Ron Preston, e-mail correspondence.
44. *Morning Oregonian*, September 25, 1911, 10.
45. David Anderson, "The Willamette Valley and Coast Railroad," Abandoned Rails, http://www.abandonedrails.com/Willamette_Valley_and_Coast_Railroad.

46. *Timberman* 12, no. 10 (August 1, 1911): 21.
47. Nixon, *Cherry Grove.*
48. *Morning Oregonian*, February 2, 1910, 8.
49. *Morning Oregonian*, February 4, 1910, 10.
50. Charlton, *Railway Car Builders*, 1957.
51. Mid-Continent Railway Museum, "Builders of Wooden Railway Cars," North Freedom, Wisconsin, http://www.midcontinent.org/rollingstock/builders/railwaystorbat.htm.
52. *Morning Oregonian*, February 2, 1910, 8.
53. *Proceedings of the American Electric Railway Engineering Association* 10 (1912): 699.
54. *Railway Age Gazette*, November 22, 1912, 13.
55. *Morning Oregonian*, January 12, 1913, 9.
56. State Rail Planner Robert I. Melbo, Oregon Department of Transportation, e-mail correspondence with author, including scanned letters.

CHAPTER 5

57. *Morning Oregonian*, April 3, 1890.
58. Michelle L. Dennis, Avery-Helm National Register of Historic Places Registration, National Park Service, 1999, 4.
59. Reynolds, *Corvallis in 1890.*
60. *Morning Oregonian*, December 25, 1889.
61. *Corvallis Gazette*, June 27, 1890.
62. *Corvallis Gazette*, September 12, 1890.
63. Ibid.
64. Ibid., November 21, 1890.
65. Reynolds, *Corvallis in 1890.*
66. *Sunday Oregonian*, February 11, 1900.
67. City of Corvallis, Ordinance 1912-374.
68. *Electric Traction* (June 1913): 318.
69. *Morning Oregonian*, December 25, 1914.

CHAPTER 6

70. *Eugene Register-Guard*, May 3, 1936.
71. *American Street Railway Investments*, 80.
72. Minor, "Archaeological Assessment of Eugene Street Railway," 7.

73. Ibid., 17.
74. *Sunday Oregonian*, March 18, 1900, 6.
75. *Morning Oregonian*, April 20, 1908, 14.
76. *Morning Oregonian*, December 20, 1909, 13.
77. *Morning Oregonian*, February 9, 1910, 12.
78. Hulin, "Eugene's Trolley Car Era," 8.
79. *Morning Oregonian*, July 17, 1910, 16.
80. *Morning Oregonian*, April 20, 1908, 6.
81. *Electric Railway Journal* (July 11, 1914).
82. *Morning Oregonian*, April 17, 1908, 15.
83. *Oregonian*, December 8, 1916, 18.
84. Hulin, "Eugene's Trolley Car Era," 11.

CHAPTER 7

85. *Oregon Voter*, January 4, 1919, 47.
86. *Electrical Review* (March 3, 1906): 355.
87. *Electric Railway Journal: Electric Railway Directory and Buyers Manual*, 96.
88. Sweeney, *History of Rail Transportation*, 9.
89. *Electric Railway Journal* (January 8, 1916): 101.
90. Sweeney, *History of Rail Transportation*, 9.

CHAPTER 8

91. *Morning Oregonian*, January 13, 1906, 9.
92. *Morning Oregonian*, June 4, 1906, 12.
93. *Sunday Oregonian*, June 3, 1906, 14.
94. *Morning Oregonian*, August 10, 1906, 6.
95. *Klamath News*, "Old Linkville Trolley Pilot Recalls Past," July 6, 1938.
96. *Electric Traction Weekly* (August 21, 1909): 890.

CHAPTER 9

97. *Electric Railway Journal* (April 11, 1914): 855.
98. Webber and Webber, *Railroading in Southern Oregon*, 73.
99. *Medford Sun*, October 6, 1915.

100. Webber and Webber, *Single Track to Jacksonville*, 80.
101. Mills, "Recent History of Oregon's Electric Interurbans," 114.
102. Webber and Webber, *Railroading in Southern Oregon*, 67.
103. *Electric Railway Journal* 42 (June 14, 1913): 1,313.
104. *McGraw Transit Directory*, 127.
105. *Moody's Manual of Railroads and Corporation Securities*, 1917, 1,095.
106. *Morning Oregonian*, February 15, 1913, 7.
107. *Jacksonville Review*, "Tea Kettle Engine Returns Home," June 14, 2014, jacksonvillereview.com/tea-kettle-engine-returns-home.
108. Webber and Webber, *Single Track to Jacksonville*, 94.
109. Hilton and Due, *Electric Interurban Railways in America*, 38.

CHAPTER 10

110. *Electrical Review* 46, no. 5 (1905): 216.
111. *Spokane Daily Chronicle*, June 5, 1905.
112. *Up-to-the-Times*, "City Railway System Expanding" (October 1908): 493.
113. Ibid., 494.
114. *Morning Oregonian*, March 18, 1907, 12.
115. *Morning Oregonian*, April 17 1907, 3.
116. *Up-to-the-Times*, "Walla Walla's Streetcar System" (April, 1907): 162.
117. *Morning Oregonian*, February 3, 1910.
118. *Morning Oregonian*, March 11, 1910.
119. *Morning Oregonian*, June 23 1908, 5.
120. *Electric Railway Journal* 33, no. 3 (January–June 1909): 122.
121. *Electric Railway Journal* 33, no. 21 (January–June 1909): 964.
122. *Brill's Magazine* 2 (1908): 249–50.
123. *Morning Oregonian*, January 15, 1922, 13.
124. Kooistra, "Walla Walla Valley Traction Company."
125. Ibid.
126. *McGraw Electric Railway Directory*, 1924, 190.

CHAPTER 11

127. Culp, *Stations West*, 22.
128. *Capital Journal*, March 24, 1950, 19.
129. Ben, "Salem's First Streetcar Line."

130. Ibid.
131. Labbe, *Fares, Please!*, 153.
132. *Daily Capital Journal*, July 21, 1910, 2.
133. *Daily Capital Journal*, July 2, 1910, 1.
134. Ben, "Salem's First Streetcar Line."
135. *Capital Journal*, March 24, 1950, 19.

Chapter 12

136. *Public Utilities Reports Inc.*, 1914, 1,007.
137. *Electric Railway Journal* (May 20, 1909): 265.
138. *Engineering and Contracting* 33 (February 2, 1910): 41.
139. Ibid.
140. *Electric Traction* (November 1912): 1,136.
141. *McGraw Electric Railway Directory*, 1924, 143.

BIBLIOGRAPHY

American Street Railway Investments. Elwood, IN, 1898.

Austin, Ed, and Tom Dill. *The Southern Pacific in Oregon.* Edmonds, WA: Pacific Fast Mail, 1987.

Charlton, E. Harper. *Railway Car Builders of the United States & Canada.* New York: Interurban Press, 1957.

Culp, Edwin D. *Early Oregon Days.* Caldwell, ID: Caxton, 1987.

———. *Oregon the Way It Was.* Caldwell, ID: Caxton, 1981.

———. *Stations West.* Caldwell, ID: Caxton, 1972.

Dennon, Jim. "Astoria's Streetcars (Part 1)." *CUMTUX* 9, no. 2 (Spring 1989).

———. "Astoria's Streetcars (Part 2)." *CUMTUX* 9, no. 3 (Summer 1989).

Dill, Tom, and Walter R. Grande. *The Red Electrics: Southern Pacific's Oregon Interurban.* Edmonds, WA: Pacific Fast Mail, 1994.

Electric Railway Journal: Electric Railway Directory and Buyers Manual. New York: McGraw, 1908.

Grande, Walter R. *The Northwest's Own Railway: Spokane, Portland & Seattle Railway and its Subsidiaries*. Vol. 2, *The Subsidiaries*. Portland, OR: Grande Press, 1997.

Gross, Joseph. *The Trolley and Interurban Directory*. New York: self-published, 1987.

Hilton, George W., and John F. Due. *The Electric Interurban Railways in America.* Palo Alto, CA: Stanford University Press, 1960.

Hulin, Gilbert. "Eugene's Trolley Car Era." *Lane County Historian* 18, no. 1 (Spring 1973).

Kooistra, Blair E. "Walla Walla Valley Traction Company." Transit 509—The Eastern Washington Transit Resource. https://transit509.com/2012/08/29/walla-walla-valley-traction-company.

Labbe, John T. *Fares, Please!: Those Portland Trolley Years.* Caldwell, ID: Caxton, 1980.

Maxwell, Ben. "Salem's First Streetcar Line." Salem (Oregon) Online History. www.salemhistory.net/transportation/streetcars_line.htm.

McArthur, Lewis A. *Oregon Geographic Names*. Portland: Oregon Historical Society, 1974.

McGraw Electric Railway Directory 1924. New York.

McGraw Transit Directory. New York: McGraw-Hill Publishing Company, 1918.

Mills, Randall V. "Recent History of Oregon's Electric Interurbans." *Oregon Historical Quarterly* 46, no. 2 (June 1945).

Minor, Rick. *An Archaeological Assessment of Eugene Street Railway Remains on Willamette Street, Eugene, Lane County, Oregon*. Eugene, OR: Heritage Research Associates, 2014.

Moody's Manual of Railroads and Corporation Securities. New York: Moody Manual Company, 1917.

Mullen, Floyd. *The Land of Linn.* Albany, OR: Dalton's Printing, 1971.

Nixon, Brigetta. *Cherry Grove: A History from 1852 to the Present.* American Revolution Bicentennial Commission of Oregon, 1976.

Public Utilities Reports Inc. Rochester, NY, 1914.

Reynolds, Minerva. *Corvallis in 1890*. Corvallis, OR: private printing, 1977.

Robertson, Donald B. *Encyclopedia of Western Railroad History*. Vol. 3. *Oregon Washington*. Caldwell, ID: Caxton, 1995.

Sweeney, Jessie. *History of Rail Transportation in Forest Grove, Oregon*. HI815XA Research Seminar. United States, 2012.

Thompson, Richard M. *Willamette Valley Railways*. Charleston, SC: Arcadia Publishing, 2008.

Webber, Bert, and Margie Webber. *Railroading in Southern Oregon and the Founding of Medford.* Fairfield, WA: Ye Galleon Press, 1985.

———. *Single Track to Jacksonville: The Rogue River Valley Railway and the Southern Oregon Traction Company*. Medford, OR: Webb Research Group, 1990.

INDEX

D

E

F

G

H

I

J

K

S

T

W

Y

Z

ABOUT THE AUTHOR

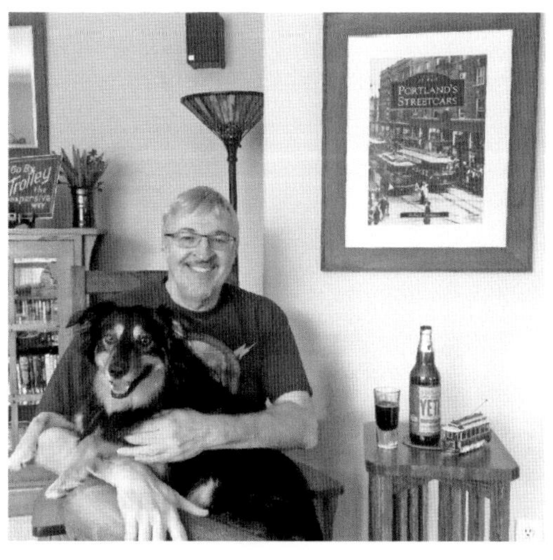

Richard Thompson is a native Oregonian whose family first settled in Linn County, Oregon, in the 1880s. His interest in street and interurban railways began as a small boy when his grandmother took him for rides on Portland's last streetcar line, to Oregon City.

A graduate of the University of Oregon, Thompson has been a trolley crew coordinator, librarian, historical museum director, archivist, college instructor and archaeological field worker. Now semi-retired, he works as a public historian, writer and consultant. Thompson is the author of six books on electric railway history and has appeared in several documentaries, including *Streetcar City*, produced by Oregon Public Broadcasting. He has also written more than a dozen entries for the online Oregon Encyclopedia.

For nearly twenty years, Richard was an active volunteer for the Oregon Electric Railway Historical Society, operating trolleys at its museum, as well as editing its newsletter and serving on the board of directors. He is also a past president of the Portland Chapter of the Victorian Society in America. He is a member of the Oregon Historical Society, the Light Rail Transit Association and the Market Street Railway.

When not doing historical research, Thompson enjoys foreign travel, ocean cruising and reading and watching mysteries. He lives in Northwest Portland with his feline assistant, Katya, and favorite visitor, Daisy.